The Art of
Bernard J. Riley

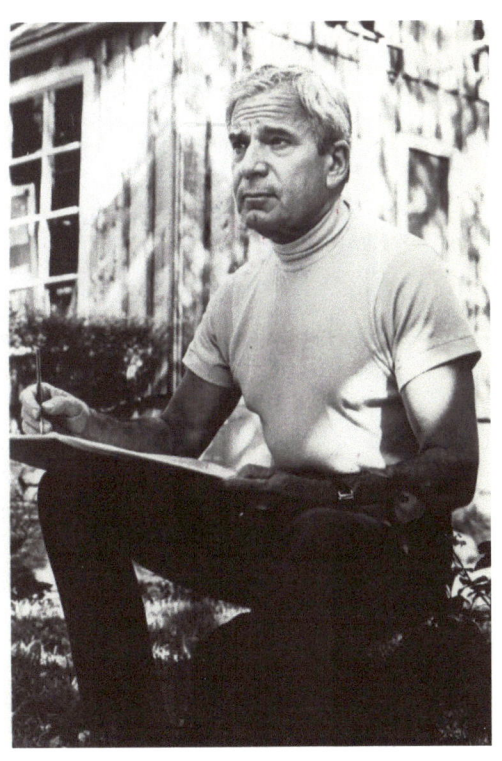

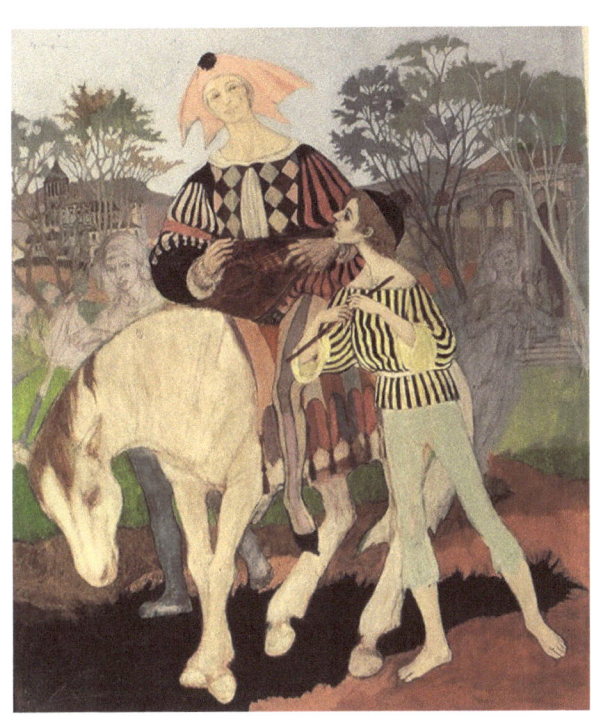

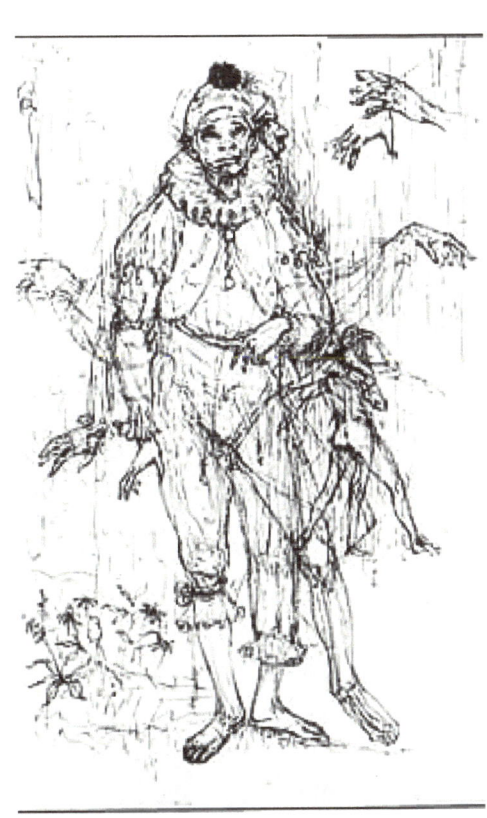

Introduction

This book was created in 2022 by John M. Riley, and is dedicated to the memory of my father, Bernard J. Riley. The book contains biographical information, photos of many of his works and some stories behind the works. Much of the information is roughly transcribed from interviews with his friend Alan Chalk, to whom I am grateful.

The intent is to have this book as a permanent record for his family, fellow artists, and researchers. Original work is currently in collections in Connecticut at the Mattatuick Museum the New Haven Paint and Clay Club, the Housatonic Art Museum, and Fairfield University. Murals are on display in Gonzaga Hall at Fairfield University and the Bridgeport Public Library. Other archives have been stored electronically and should be available by contacting the Mattatuck the Bridgeport Public Library or on line at Bernard-riley.com.

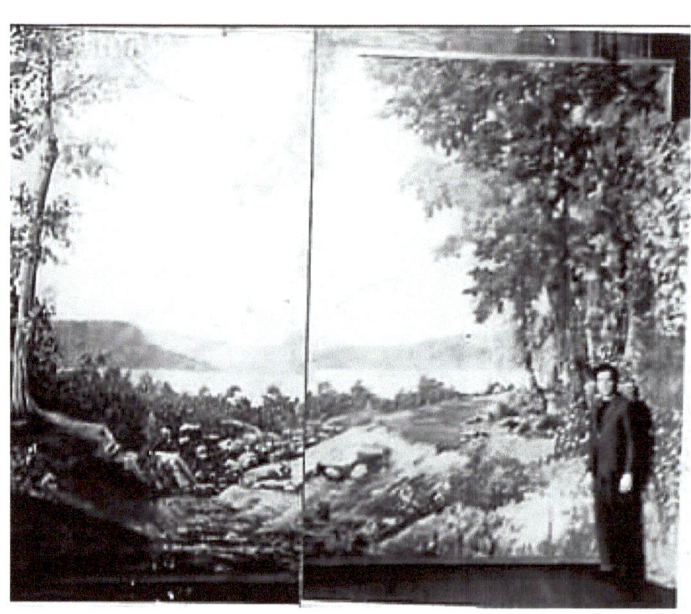

Stage set for Central High School 1930

He loved the big canvas from 1930 in high school to 1977 in the New York Times

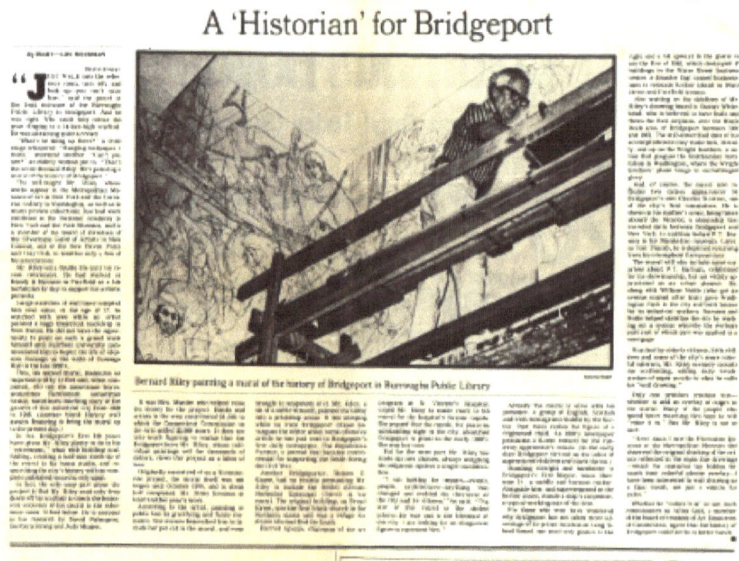

Title page: photograph of artist in front of studio 1974, detail of "The Prodigal Son" 1978, Self Portrait as a harlequin 1978

Early Life

Bernard Riley was born in 1911 and spent his childhood on the colorful streets of a proud, working-class neighborhood in Bridgeport, Connecticut. His adventurous youth resembles that of Huck Finn. The winter quarters of the Barnum and Bailey Circus was in the next block, and he managed to earn a few dollars by gilding the acrobats.

At Bridgeport's Central High School, he became an industrious designer and builder of stage sets for the school's prize-winning plays. Riley painted signs, illustrated catalogues, arranged window displays, cartooned for local newspapers, and put his hands on anything offering a creative challenge.

"I started out, I wanted very much to be a stage designer. That was the career that I had had in mind. This meant large pieces. I found this little old man on the loft in New Haven doing a backdrop for the theater. This thing must have been about 20 by 40 probably, a real tremendous piece, and here this little guy that was hardly 5 foot 6 standing in the loft doing it. This was for the stage at Roxy Hall, a society, that used to put on plays there and shows"

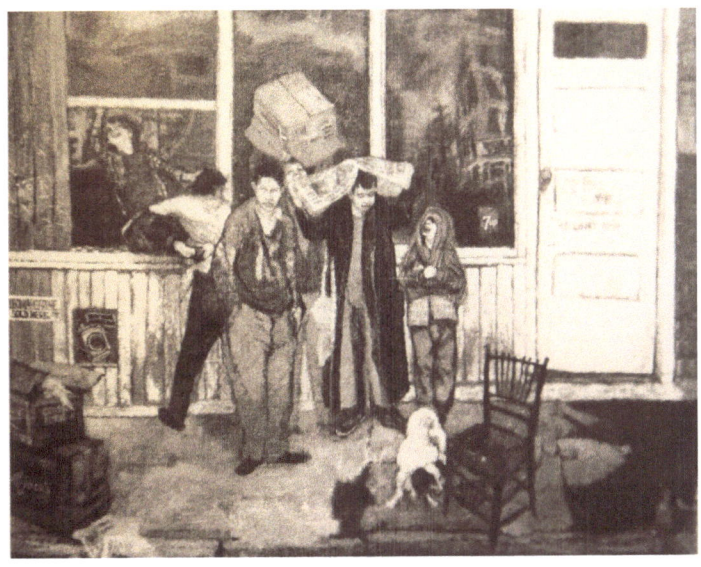

The Newsboys 1955

While he was stationed at the Philadelphia Naval Hospital during World War II, Riley taught art to returning amputees as a part of their rehabilitation. He credits the Navy for sending him to Temple University where he was trained in surgical anatomy for purposes of physical therapy. In his daily activities working with the handicapped, and from his anatomical studies with cadavers, Riley feels he gained a solid grounding in classical anatomy.

He felt lucky to land a temporary job as a lab technician during the pit of the Great Depression. He spent the next 41 years working forty hours per week at Handy and Harman in Fairfield, Connecticut, yet he managed to not sacrifice precious time for his art. For 20 years, he painted in a damp basement, until at last, in 1965, he designed and constructed a studio attached to his garage.

With no formal training, he first started painting the scenes he knew from the south side of Bridgeport - the rather tattered newsboys with their mongrel dog in front of an old building, and a short-order counter or bar lit up on a dark evening.

In 1938 he married Marie Roder; they remained married until his death. In 1948 they had a son whom they named John.

"These paintings are all related to my own environment. This is Seaside Park. As you can see it's a thunderstorm coming up. I discovered that the people seem to be at a festival and so I called it holiday."

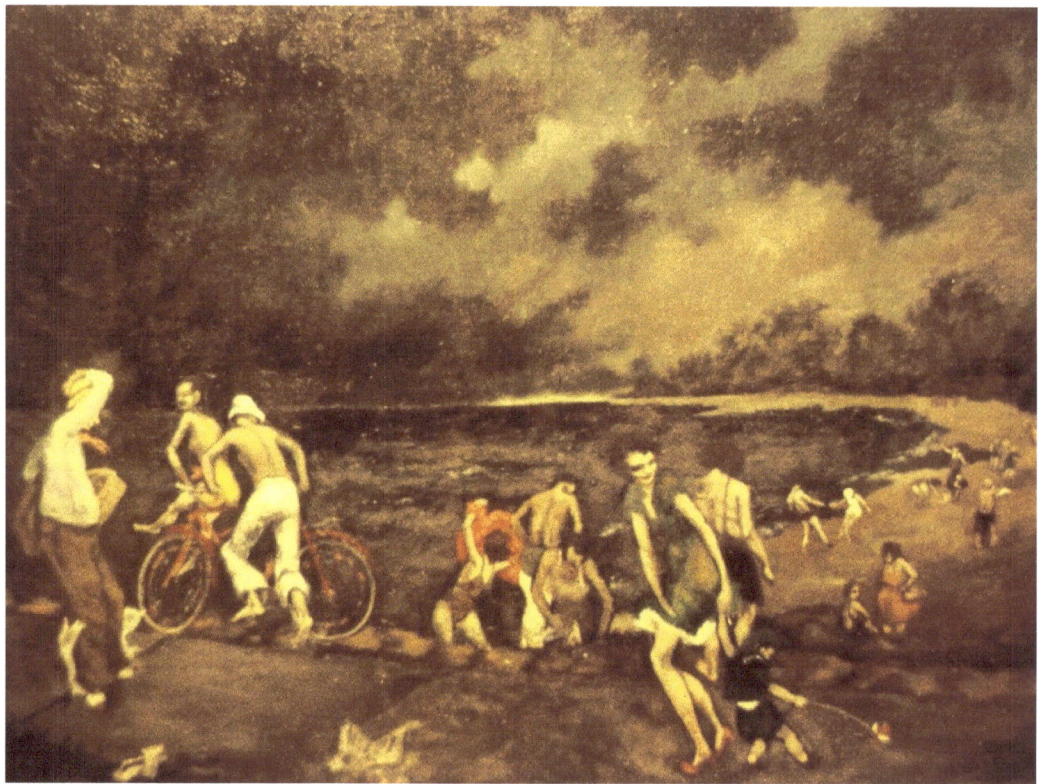

Holiday 1952

J Street 1952

"The creation of this piece was a kind of discovery for me, because here I began to realize that the picture wasn't as important to me as what was happening as I was observing and painting. The picture began to dictate to me. I found I could paint freely and without any pre-planning

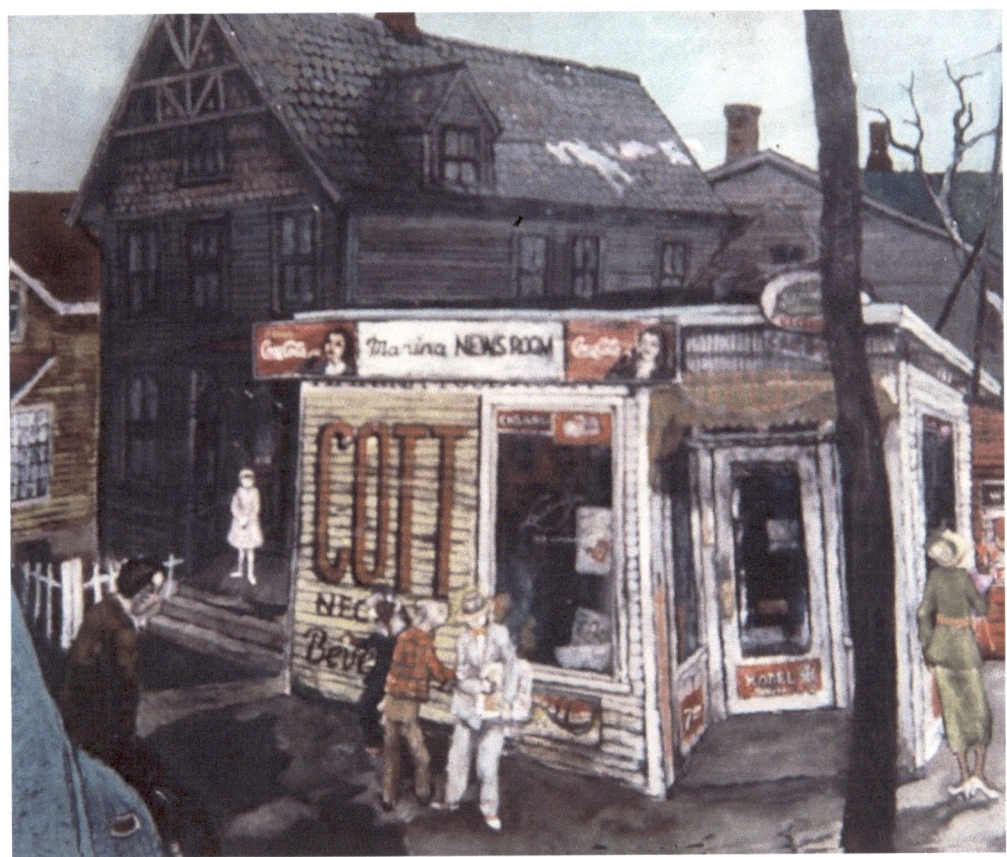

J Street 1954

This painting is part of my environment, part of the things that surrounded me. This was the corner of Johnson St. and Ridge Ave, a corner I knew well. In this case, I painted from memory. I suddenly envisioned this little figure of a girl. She looked like a little blossom with her little pink coat and white gloves on this rather grim and shabby rundown corner.

The story then began to develop in my mind. This little girl just came to be there and from that the story I thought of it as Easter Sunday. Now the little girl shows this in her brand-new clothes and bright pink. The man standing or leaning against an old beat-up car is unaware probably that it is even Easter Sunday.

The three little boys there. Two of them are dressed in ordinary everyday clothes. But the third little boy with the Sunday newspapers is dressed partly for Easter Sunday too. And the lady walking around the corner on Ridge, with a pot of flowers; also, part of the Easter Sunday scene."

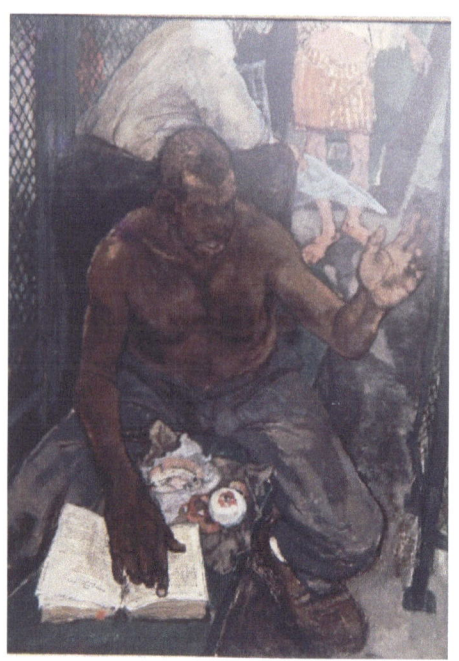

Not in Bread Alone, 1955

"This was a man that was well over 6 foot tall and weighed well over 200 pounds. And I worked with him at Handy and Harman and Fairfield. He used to sit in what we call the changing room and have his lunch there and he always had the Bible with him. And if you passed by him, he would just hold you up and he'd preach from the Bible. And I, I've just sort of picked up the title of not in bread alone from that. He has really a very, very nice man and unfortunately died at a very early age. This painting was in the collection of Corcoran Museum in Washington D.C."

Not in Bread Alone 1955

Painting of men awaiting execution in Cuba shortly after Castro came to power. The painting was purchased by Washington D.C. court.

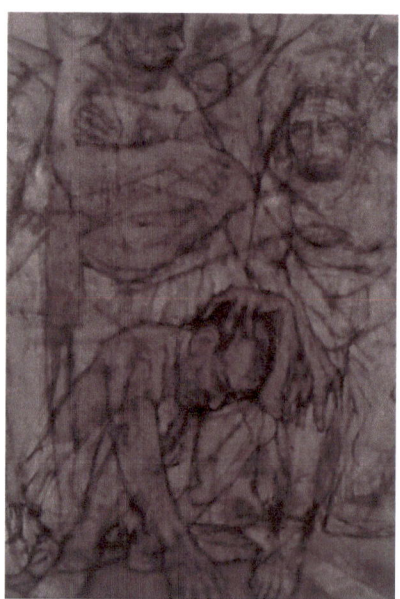

Seven Men Waiting 1960

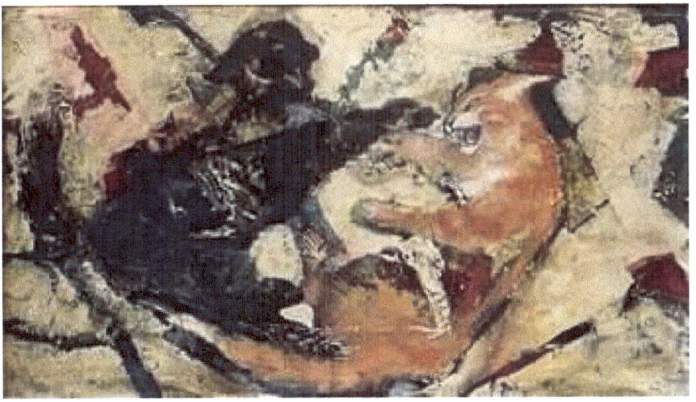

Black and Tan 1954

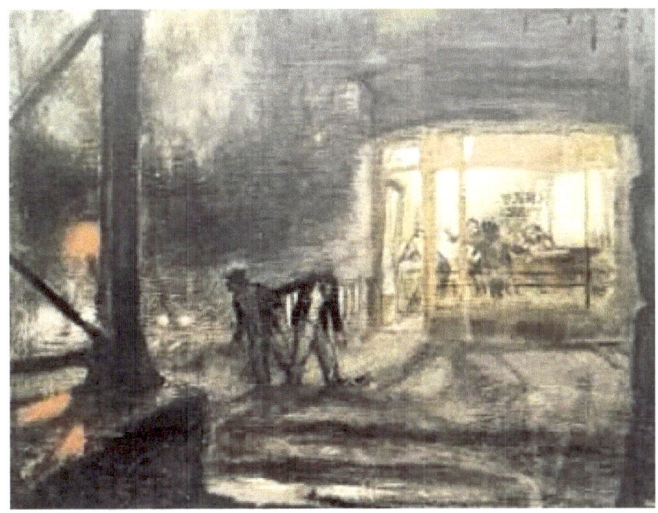

Park Rest 1954

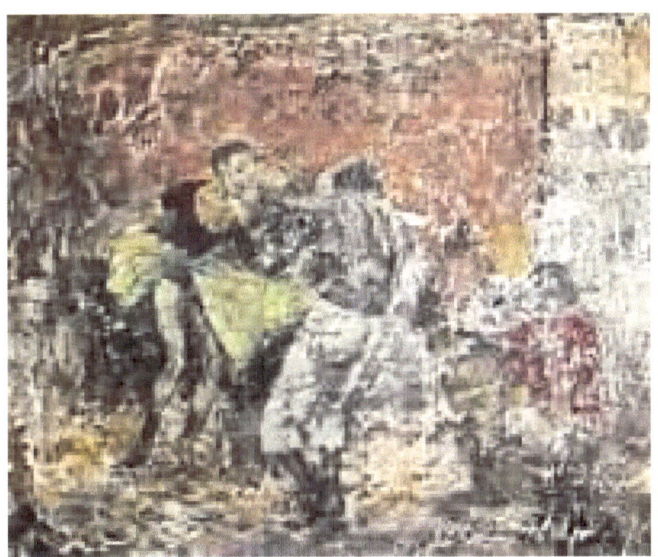

Cooch Dancer 1952

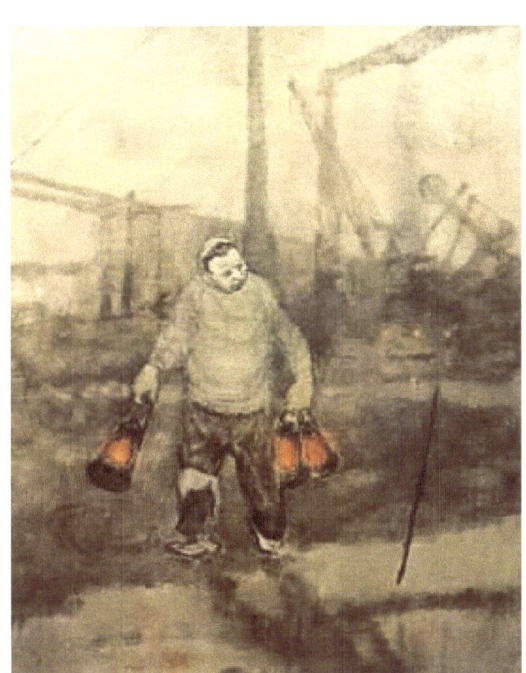

Night Watchman 1955

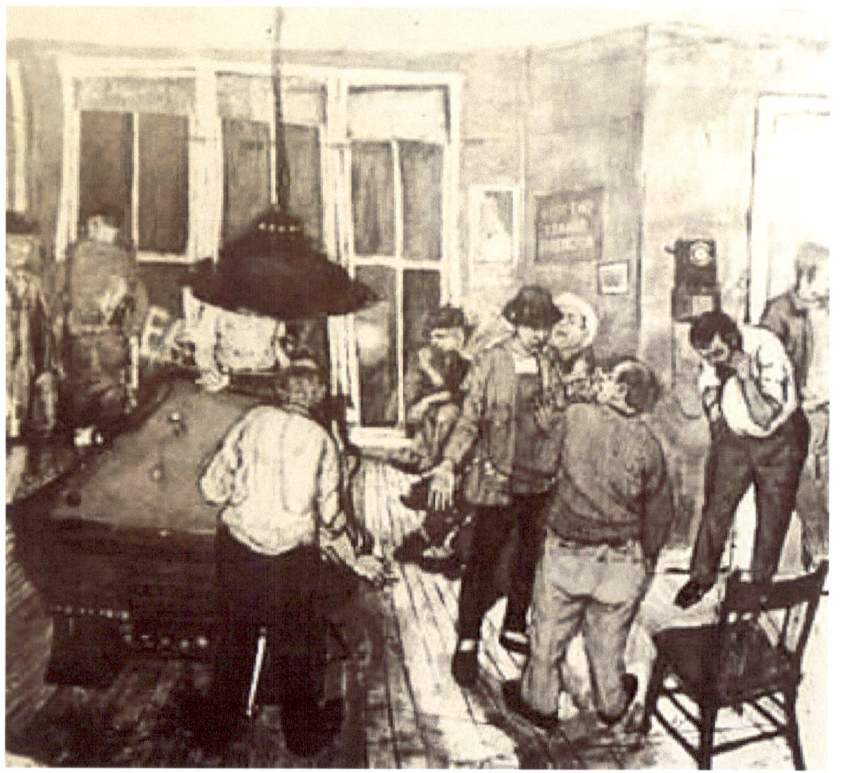

Worcester Poolroom 1954

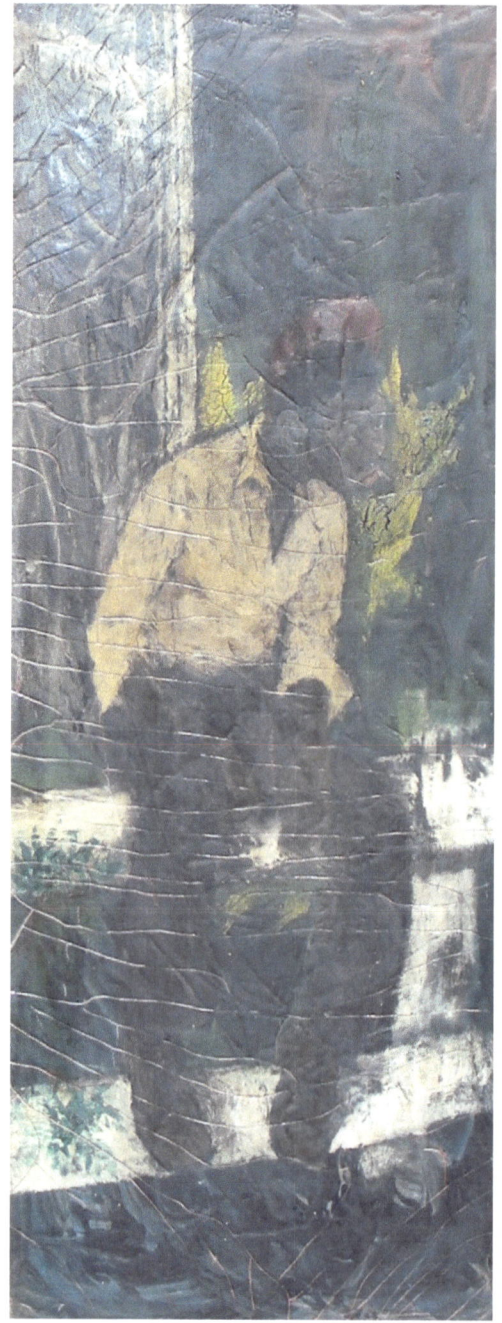

Willie 1953

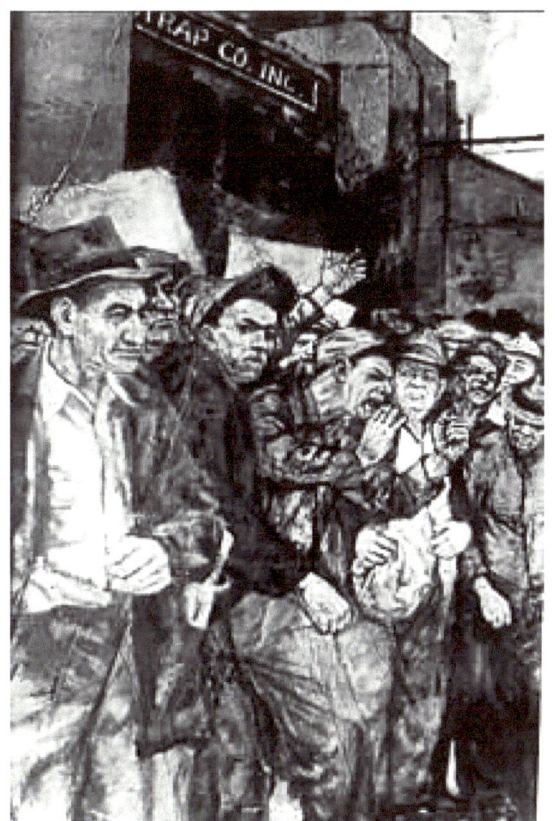

The Strikers 1954

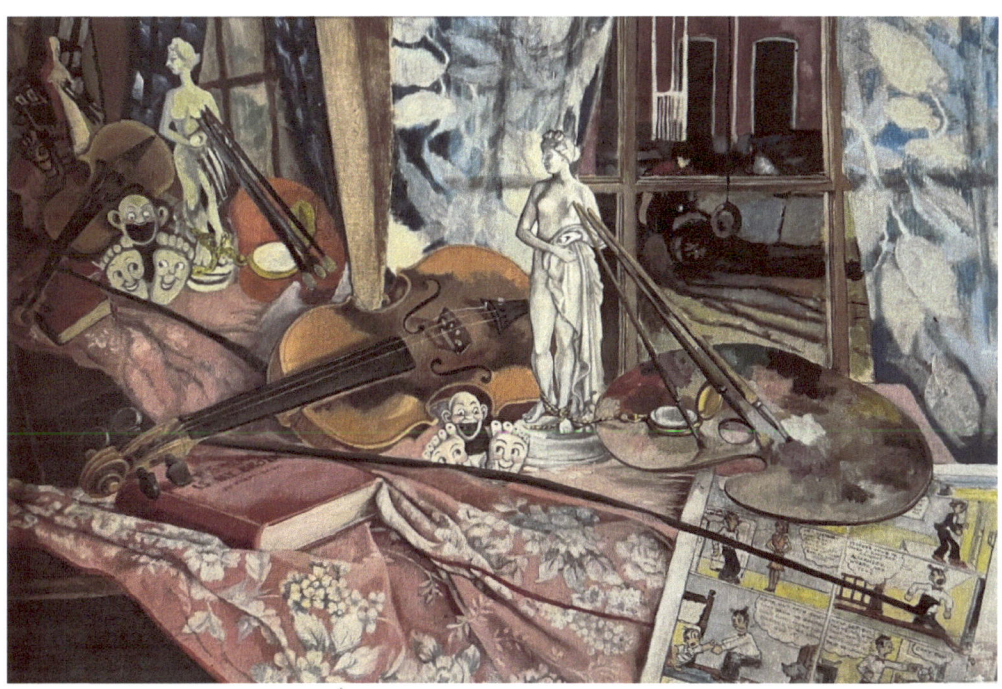

Sunday Comic 1942

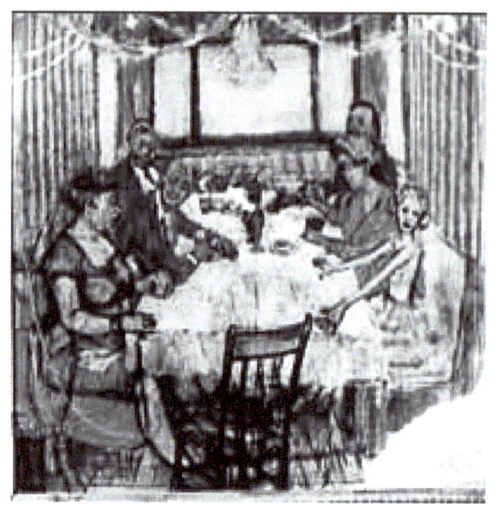
Wedding Party 1961

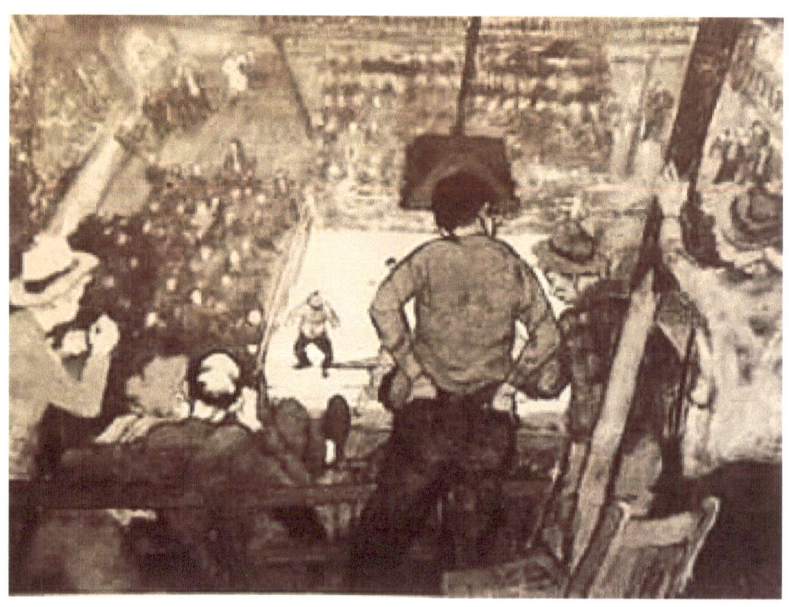
Durwins Arena 1946

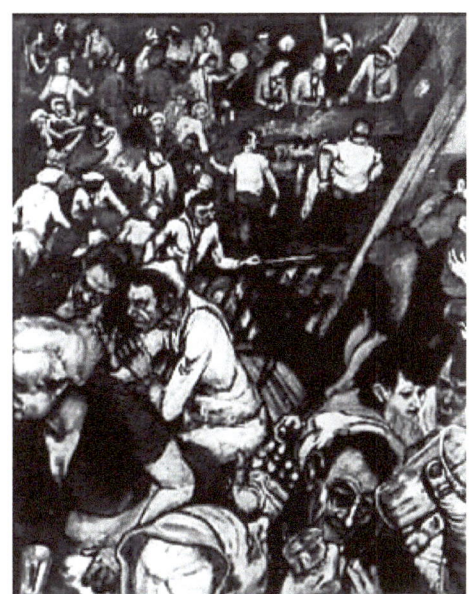

Here's to Mcginnin 1942

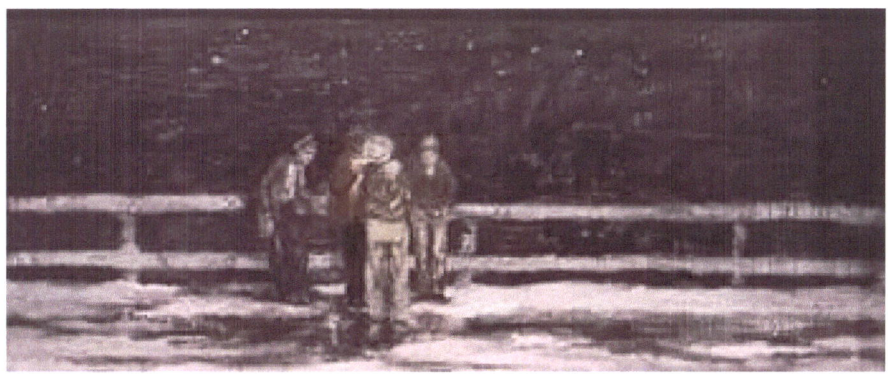

Night Shift 1952

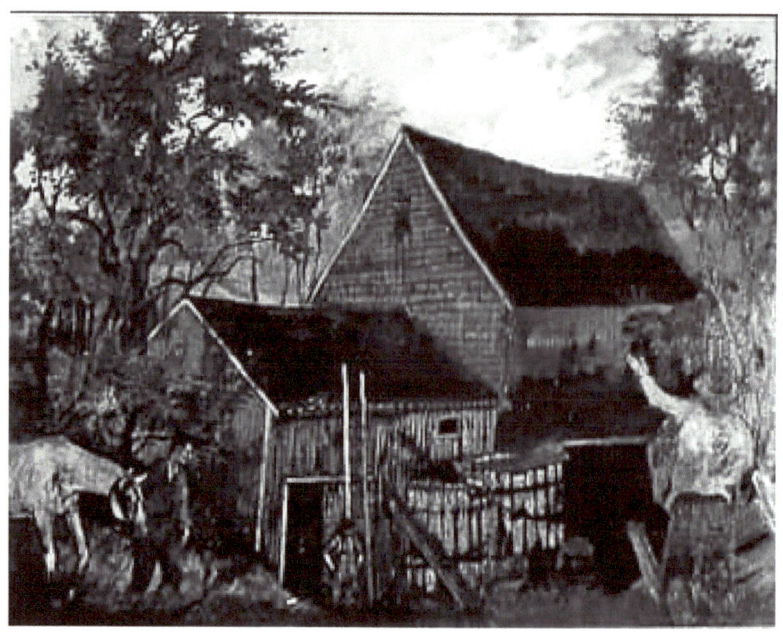

Perry's Mill 1950

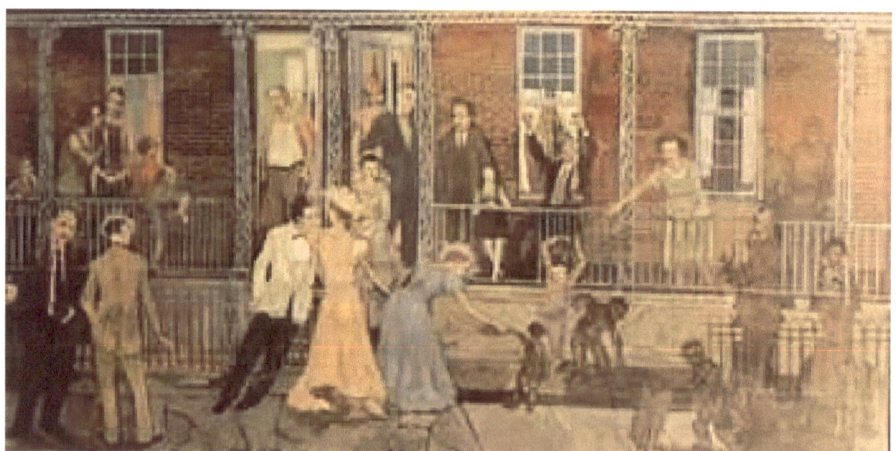

Wedding in Warren Court 1959

Early Figure Painting

I've always been interested in tattooed people. I've been interested in the tattoo and the design of the tattoo itself.

This is a South Pacific native. The tattoos on this man's body are identifications of his answers. These particular designs that were tattooed on the body may be family identifications that came down through

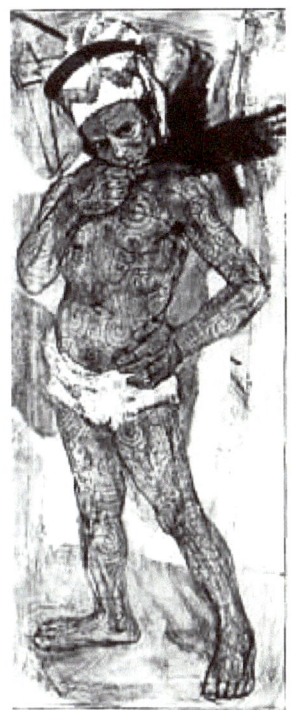
Tattooed Man 1958

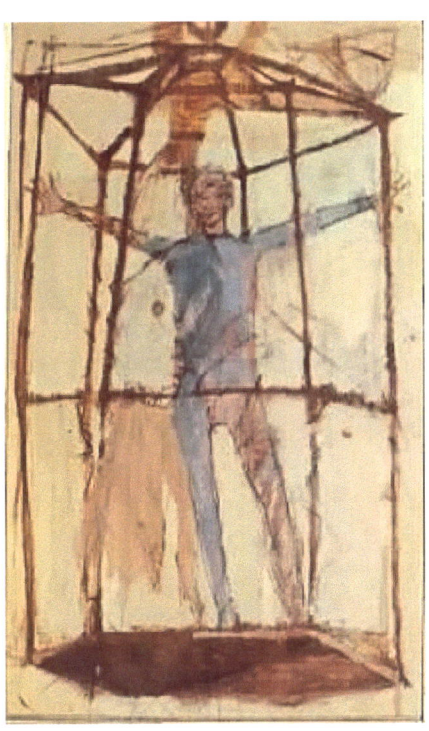
Man in a Cage 1961

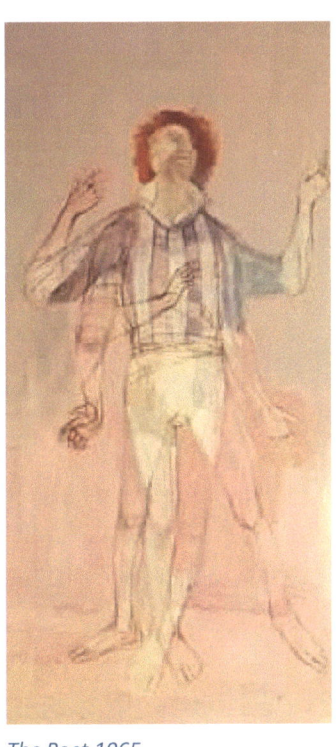
The Poet 1965

generations. And a certain design meant a certain relationship to a family.

Reviewing a Riley art exhibition, art critic Martha Scott stated: "One surmises he studied drawing and anatomy at the National Academy, that he was exposed to the frescoes and gilding techniques of Florence, that he soaked up the treasures of the Uffizi Palace.... No conjecture about an artist could be more erroneous!"

A long-standing affiliation with the Silvermine Guild of Artists in New Canaan, Connecticut began when he first exhibited there in 1951. He was later elected to the Board of Trustees and was made a Guild Fellow; the organizations highest honor. By that time, Bernard Riley was established as a a major artist in the area.

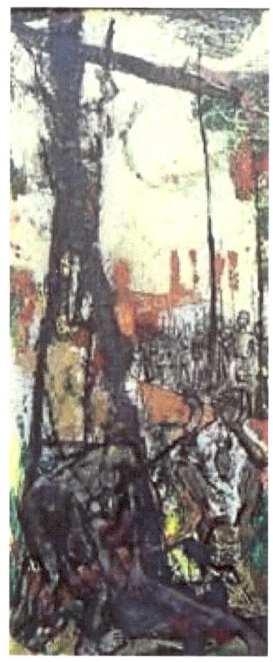

Man on a Ladder 1957

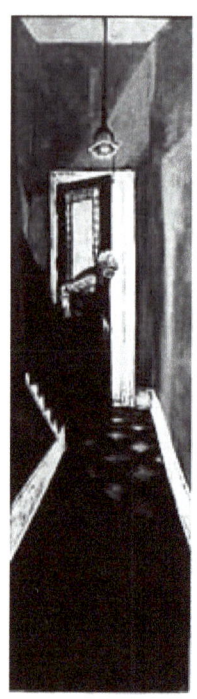

Uncle Joe 1956

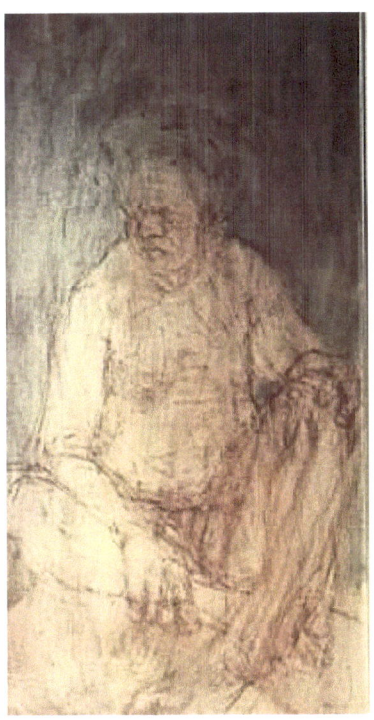

Man on Beach 1960

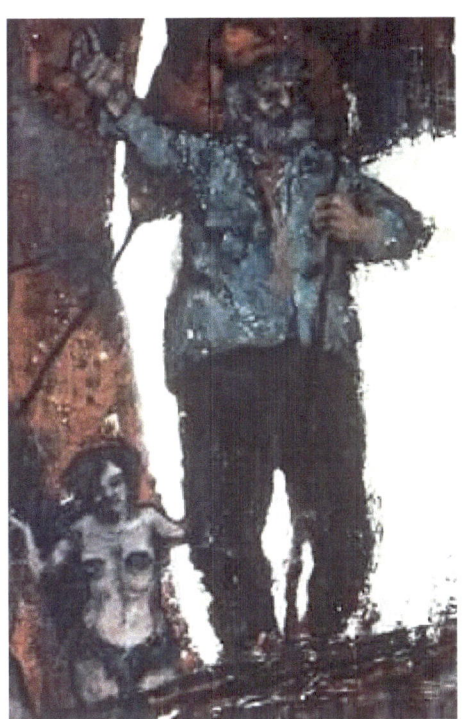

The Barker 1954

In 1958, Riley received national recognition through an article in American Artist magazine. In that article, Riley described his love for art: "each painting is an adventure for me. I paint solely for the joy or excitement of painting and, as we all know, enjoyment comes almost entirely from anticipation or expectancy, rather than from realization. I like to feel that as I proceed, I may encounter an open door to unknown painting possibilities. Entering these doors and exploring the territory within, feeling my way through experimentation, I am accorded the delightful thrill that comes of discovery. Thus, each painting becomes an entirely new venture, and the pattern of achievement may vary in each case.

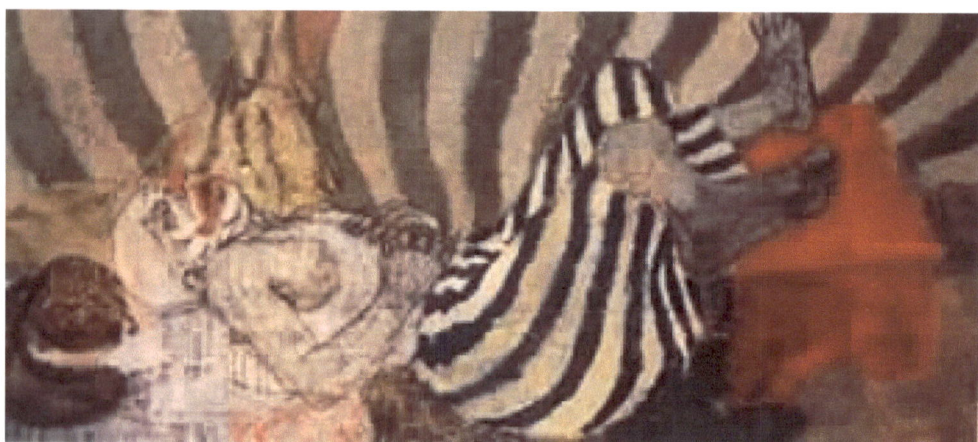

Sleeping Clown, 1960

The reason I was so interested in clowns and Harlequins and that sort of thing is I was born and grew up just within two blocks of the circus winter quarters. The clown always appeared to me to be the earthy smell and character of the circus. He might have been the low man on the totem pole, he might have been the last in the pecking order, but still he had the character of what I felt the circus was all about.

Now here in this case, I feel that this sleeping clown becomes sort of a chameleon. He's absorbed the color surrounding him. The stripes of the tent behind them, the stripes of his trousers, all sort of meld together, and bring him in.

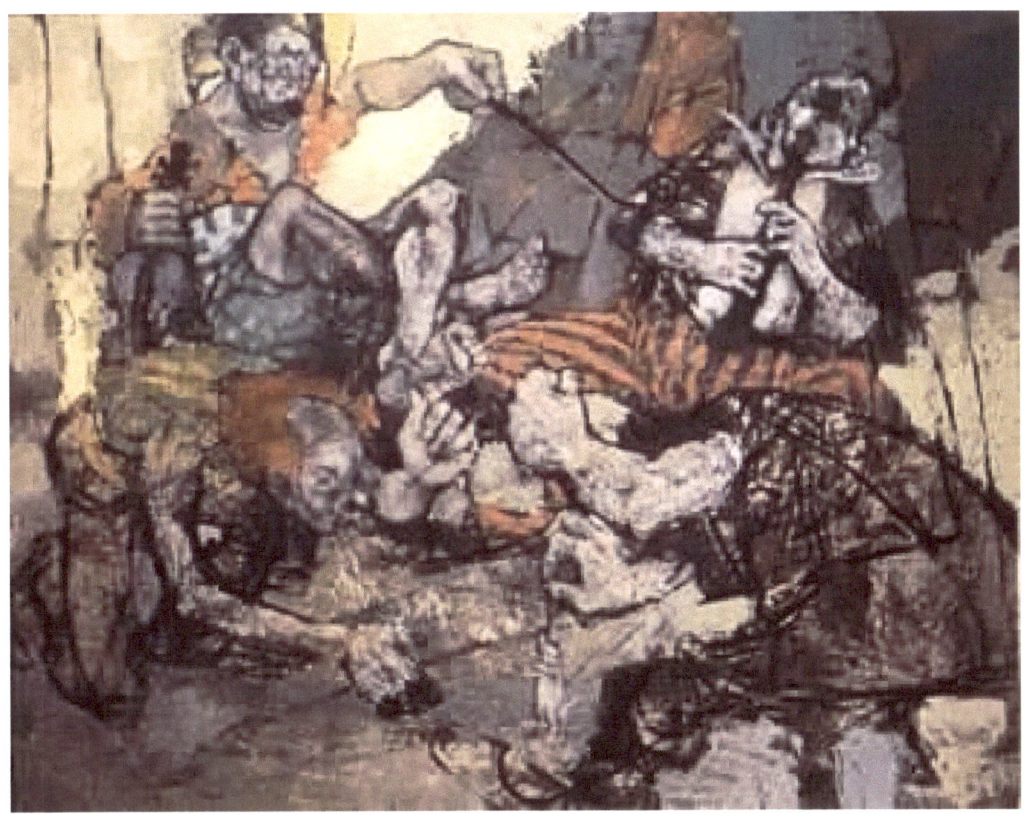

Dancing Mouse, 1960

The clowns I began to create, just simply draw; none of this work has any pre sketching. And there's no pre concept of the content.

The work begins and they're alone. It's sketched out there whatever happens, happens purely by accident.

Now here we had these clowns, the three of them, especially the one in the upper left playing a violin, a very innocent sort of clown person. One that you wouldn't take offence at, one that was a happy sort of person, and the other fellow with the flute. No problem with him. You're not concerned with what he's thinking. The man in the lower left is involved with this rather large, bizarre figure that might not even be a clown, and is dressed in some rather odd clothing. He has large, powerful hands. And from his hands dangled this little innocent mouse.

Multiple Image Period

Man with a Wounded Bird, 1958

This is the first major work involving the Multiple Image technique

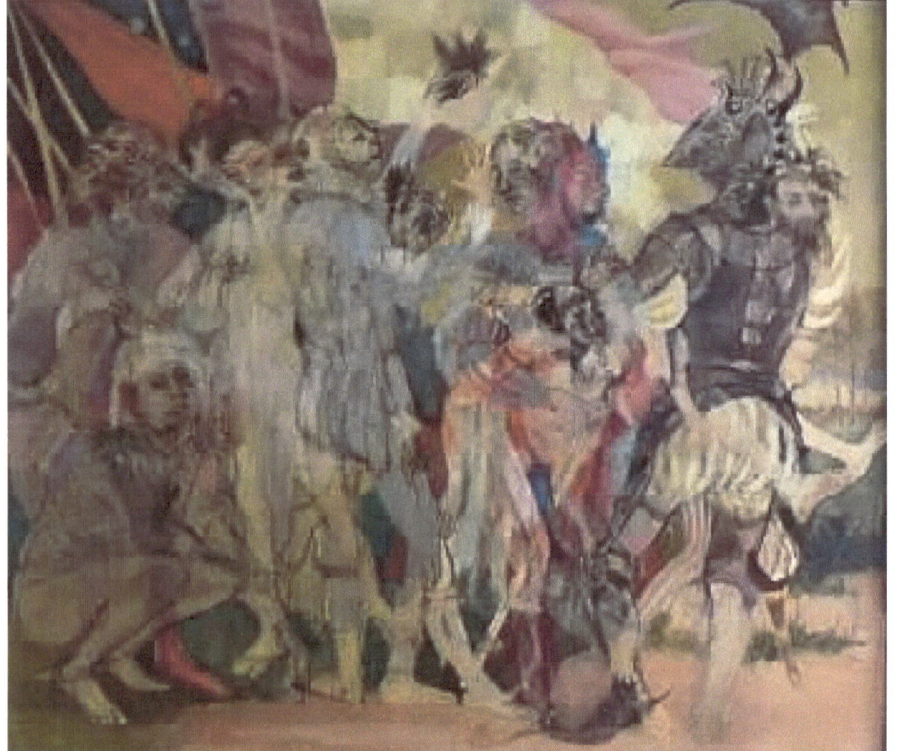

The Man with a Wounded Bird, 1958

As his art matured, he developed a unique style of multiple image. He described it in this manner: "We never really see a person in static form. We remember them in a multiple image. I am attempting to show this difference in time, to get an intellectual depth rather than the depth of a draftsman. The idea of painting pictures with multiple images first came through drawing and correcting. Part of the plan is to create intrigue and excitement. Things tend to be dull when they are static. Here ones curiosity is aroused. What is occurring?

This is an image, not necessarily in motion, but an image that is changing. Changing it in one sense in motion. Another sense in emotion; change of attitude or personality.

This began simply the same as all the others purely drawing on the Masonite, just starting off with no plan, no special looking forward to anything but just the seeking out the mystery of it all. Just the excitement of something happening while you're actually making these marks.

It's just like one thread leading to another. For this Harlequin it was the motion of the head.

`Hands were the things that interested me about the change. Put it that the restlessness of this particular figure. He's the only one in the beginning in this panel. And it had some kind of thing in his hand in the first few brush marks. And then these brush marks looked like a bird. And so a bird evolved out of it. These few quick brush marks.

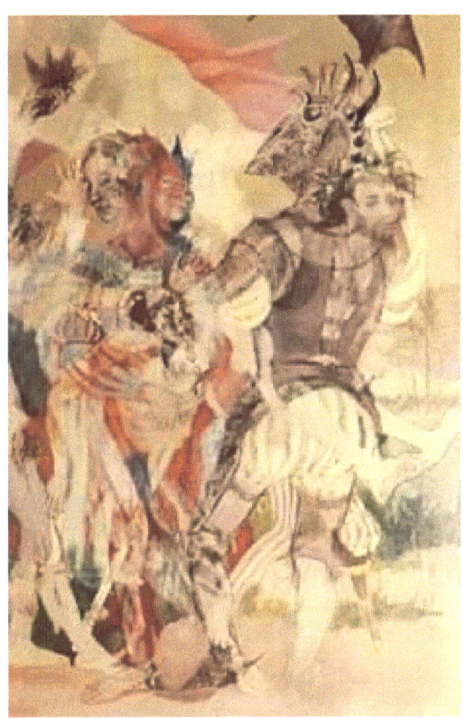

The second figure came to be a man in armor. The armor again came about accidentally, but it began to work out. I felt that here I had a figure of a warrior. In contrast to a figure of a Harlequin, that is, that's as far as any kind of thinking went.

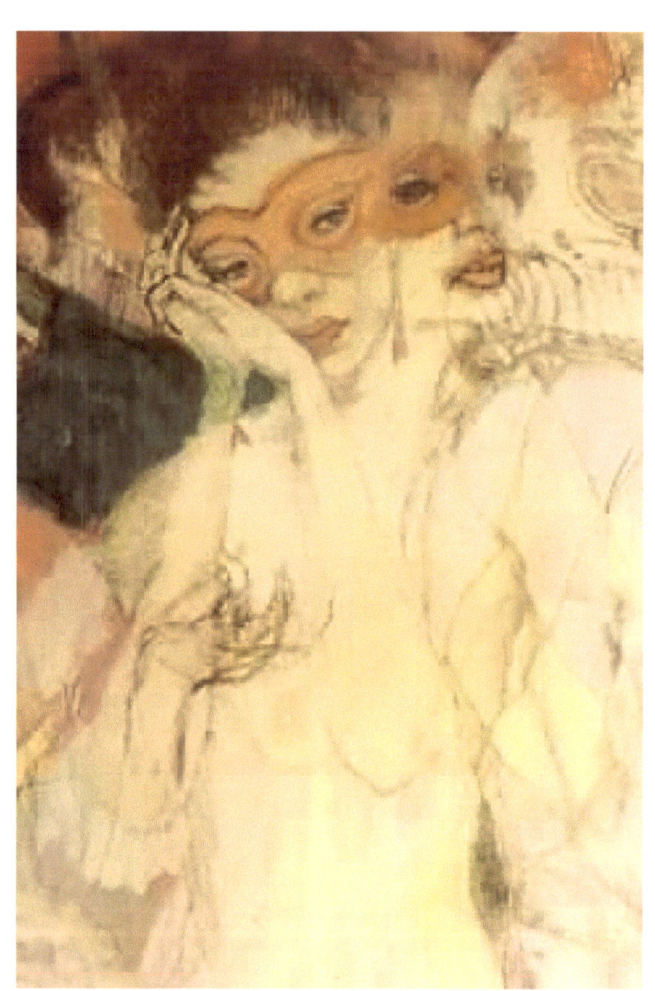

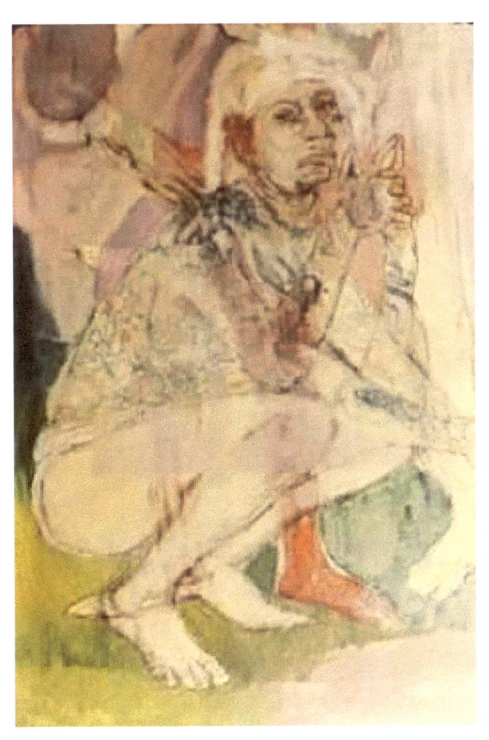

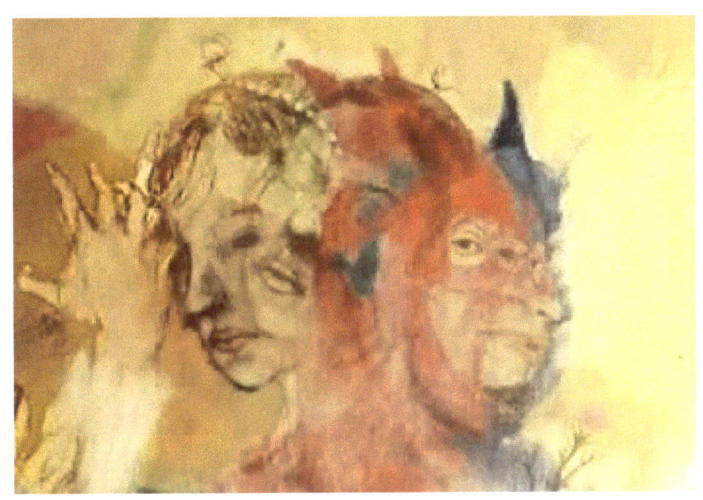

Through his career Bernard Riley created more than 200 works , the following pages illustrate many of them -

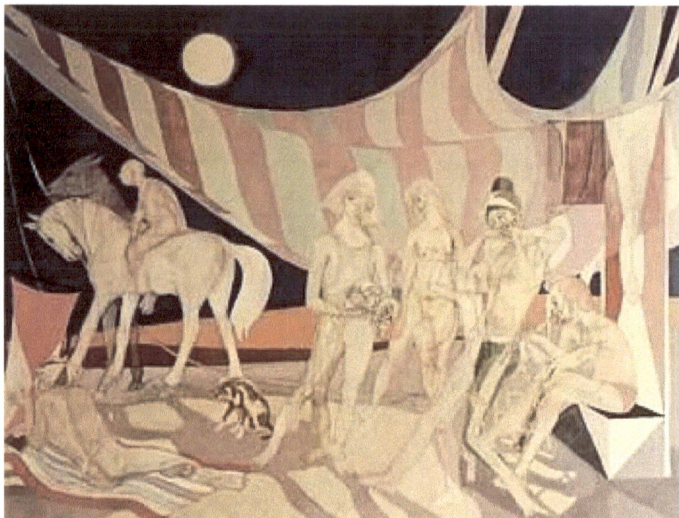

Lament to a Spotted Dog 1960

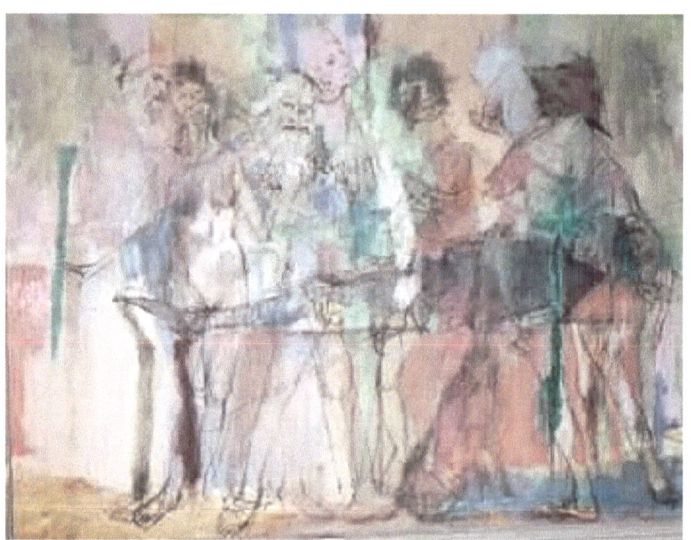

Rehearsal for a Greek Tragedy 1970

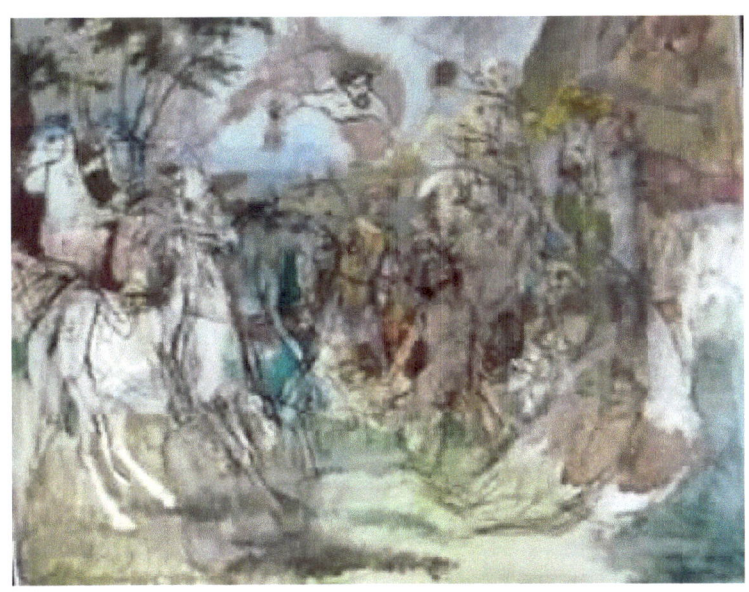
1Conversion of St Paul 1978

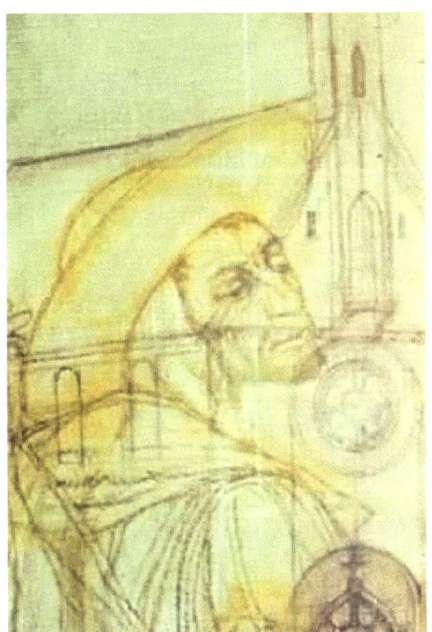
St. Vincent 1983

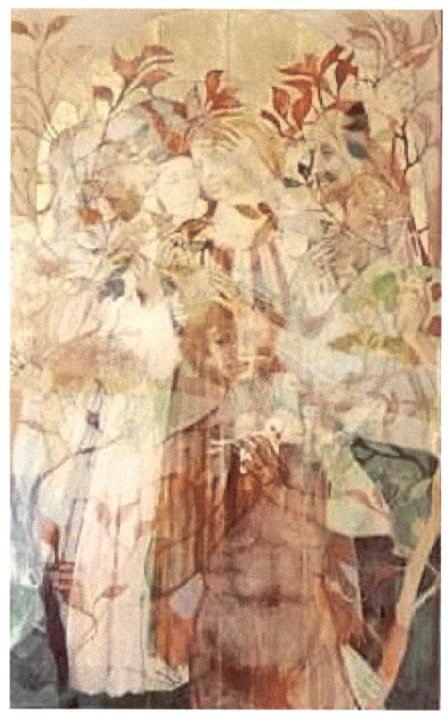

Young Man of Assisi 1979

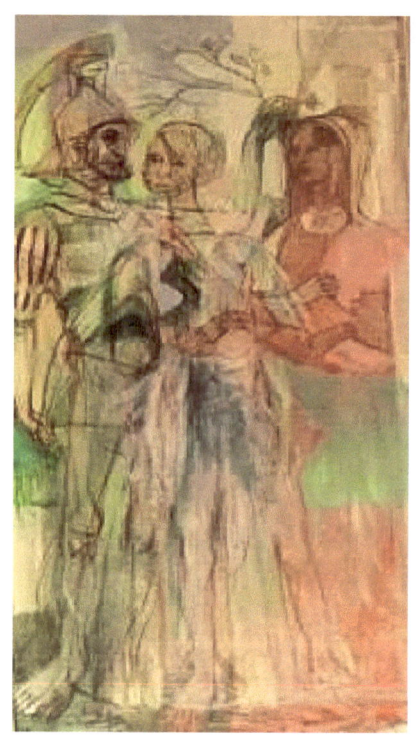

Warrior in the Garden 1965

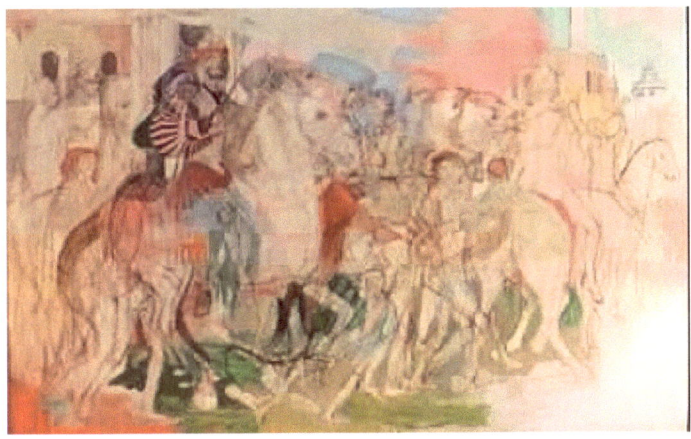

Charles VII Entering Paris 1967

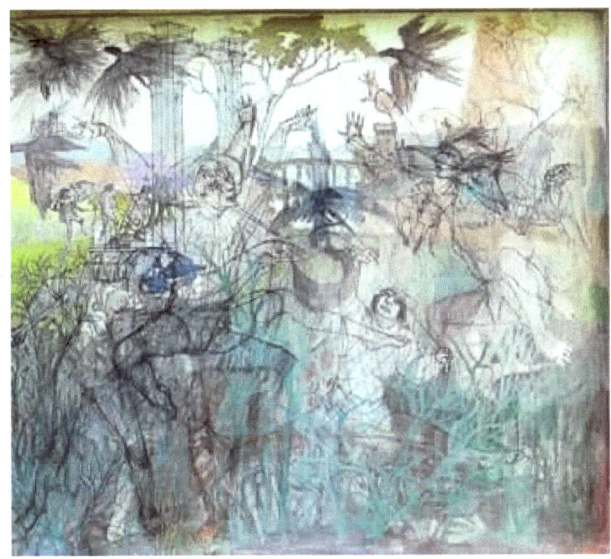

Crows in the Cornfield 1980

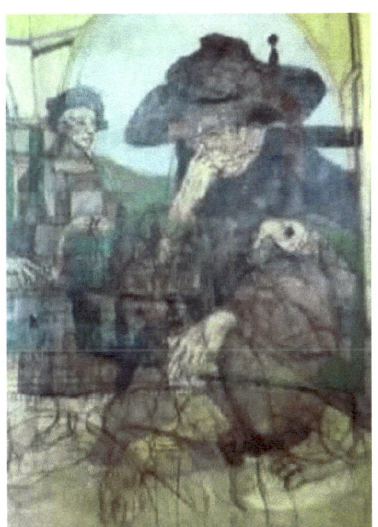

St. Anthony Playing Chess with the Devil 1965

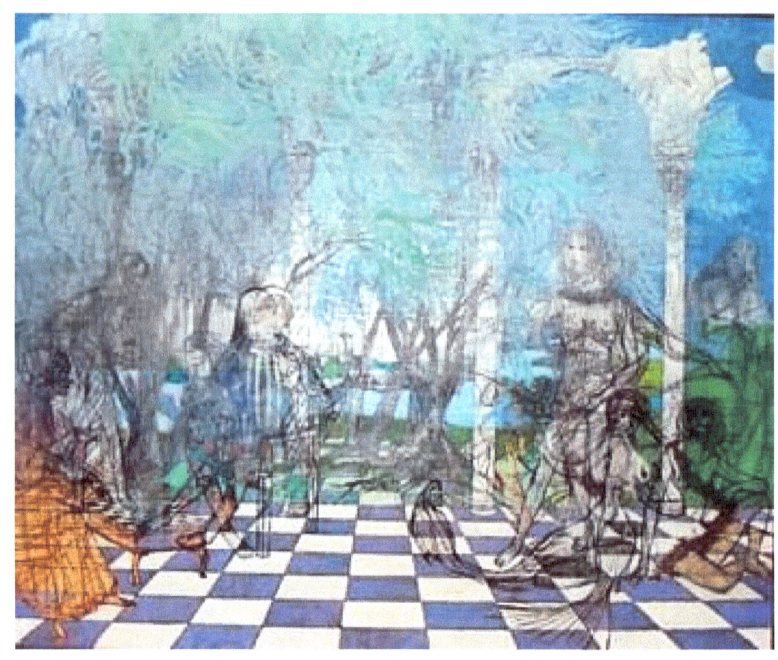

The Willow Garden 1982

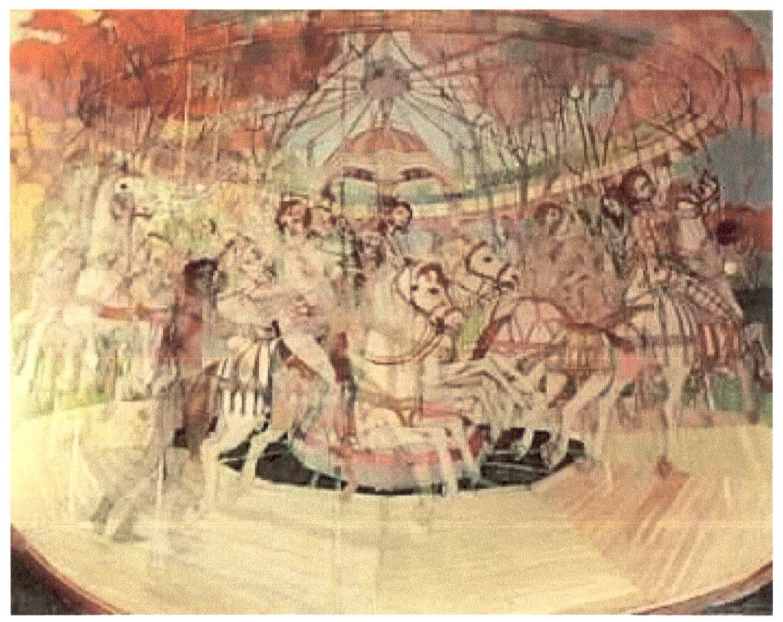

The Carousel 1967

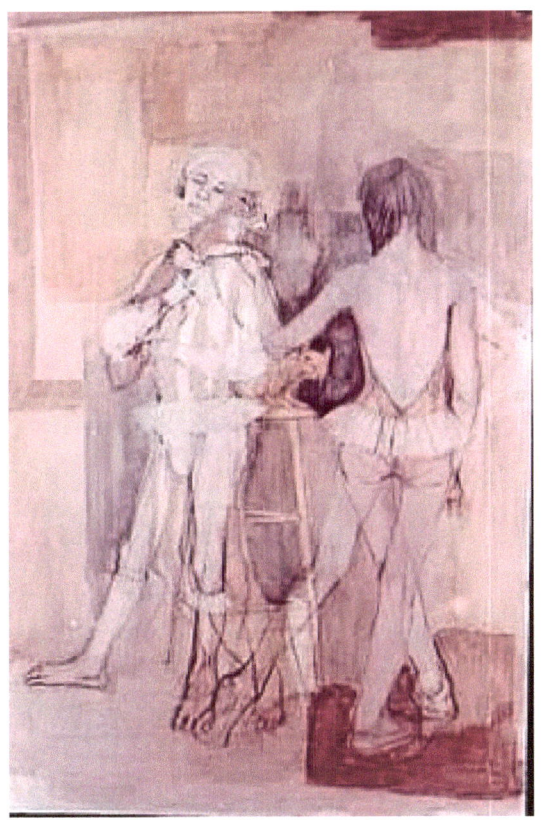

Harlequin with a Ballerina 1970

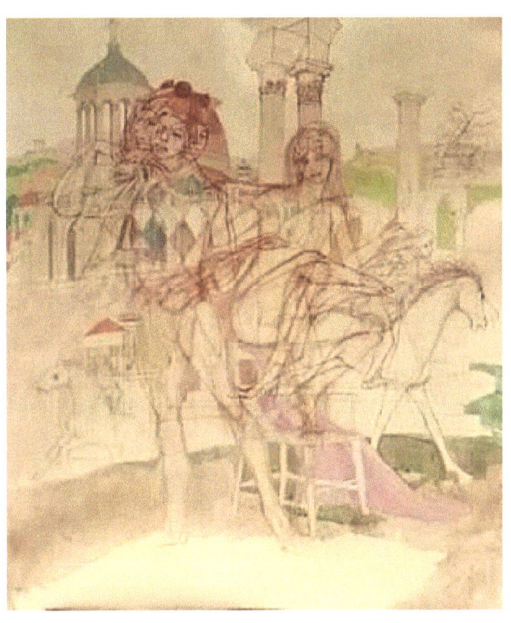

Details of a Roman City 1980

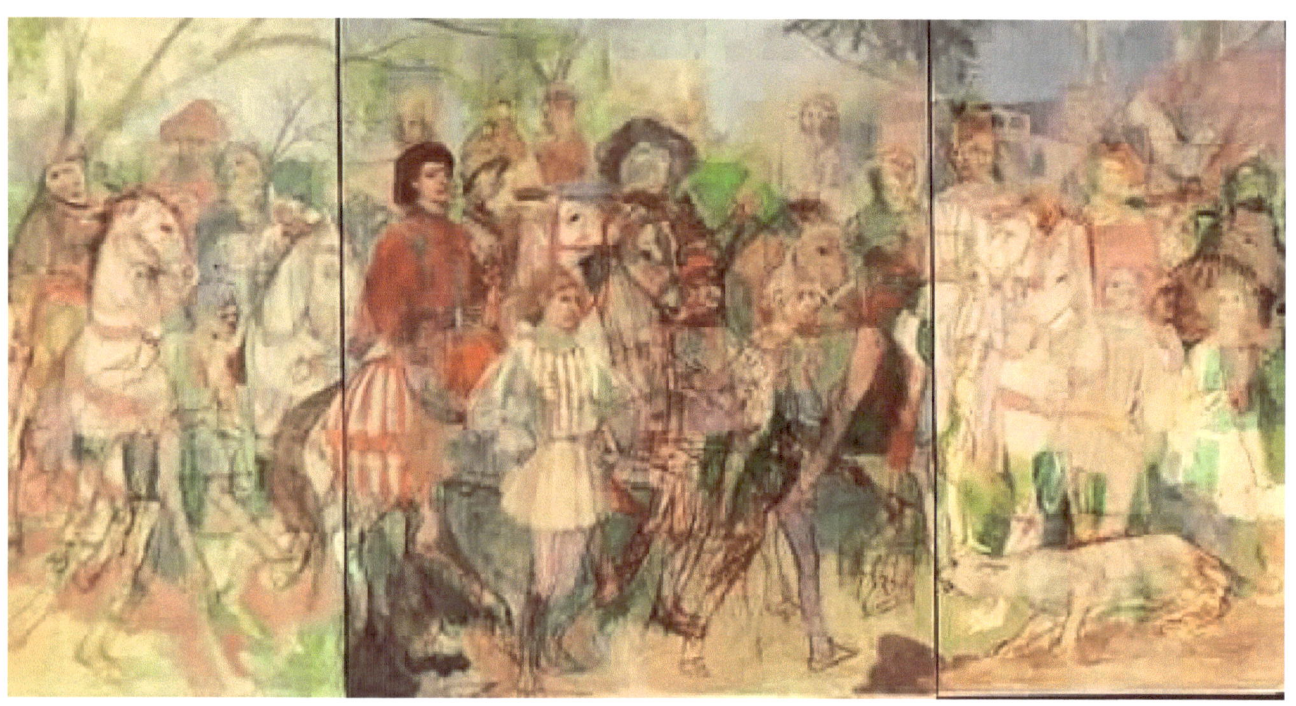

Homage to the Medici 1979

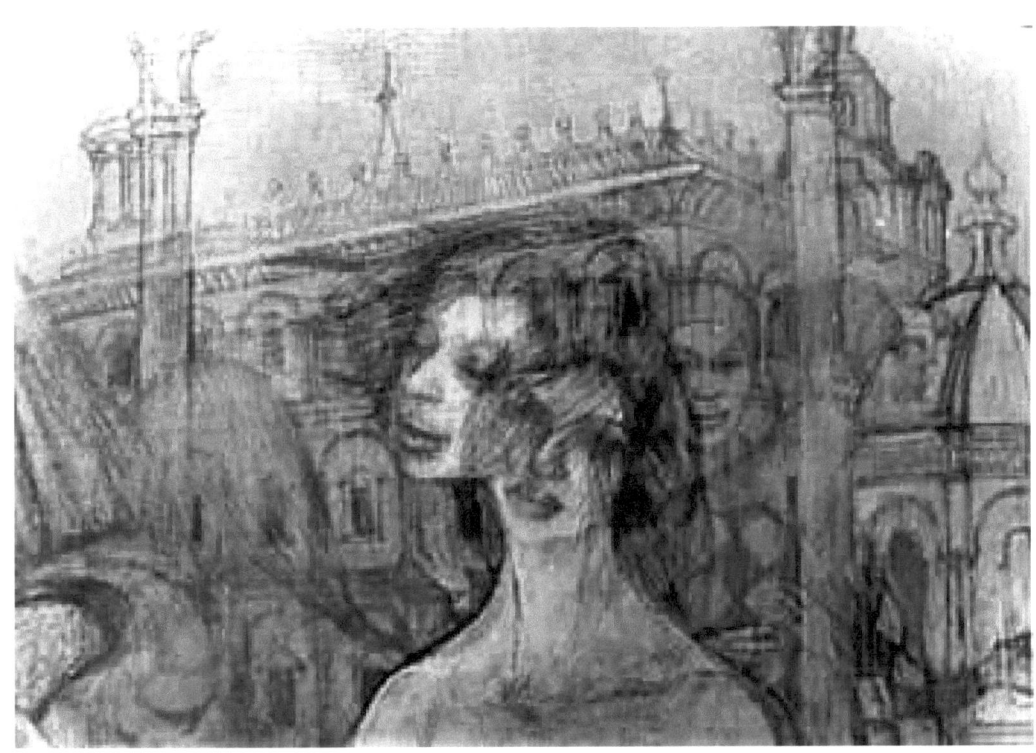

Life of St, Giles 1980

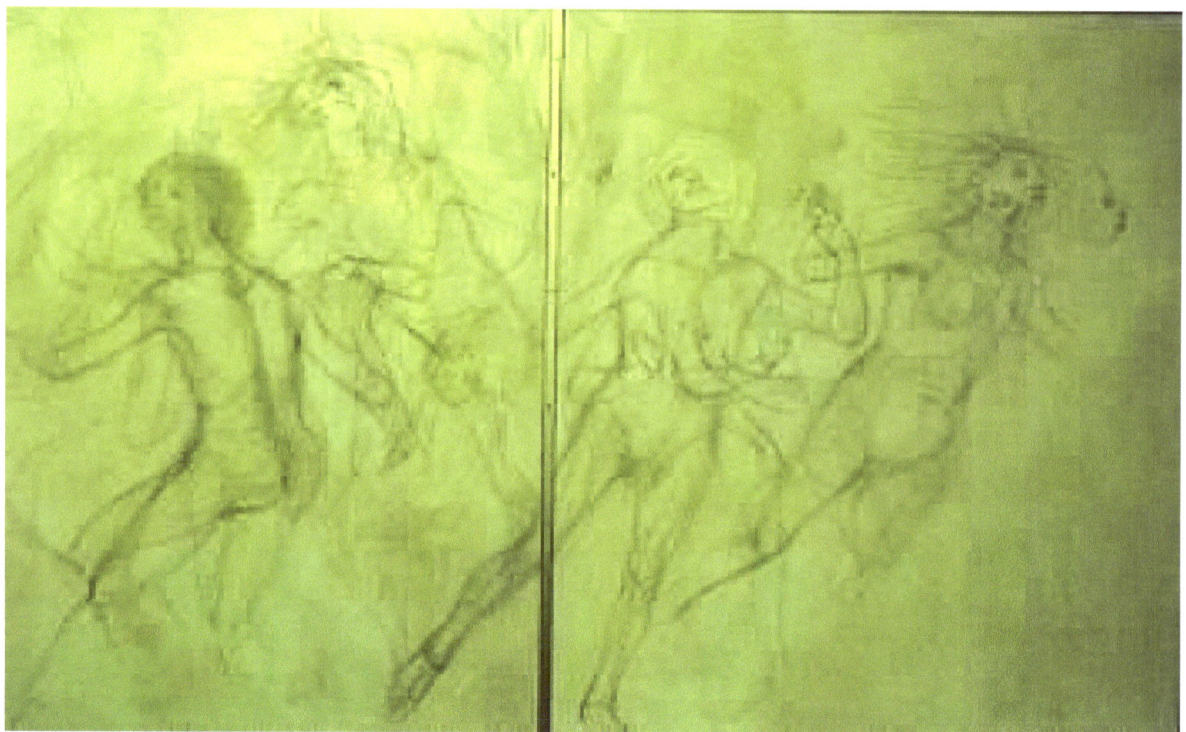

The Garden # 2 1974

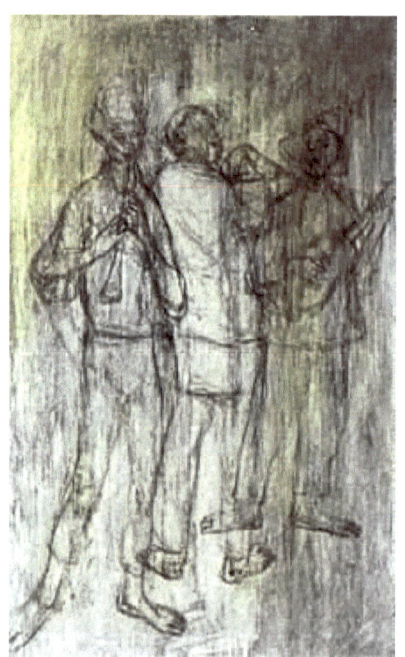

Three Musicians 1960

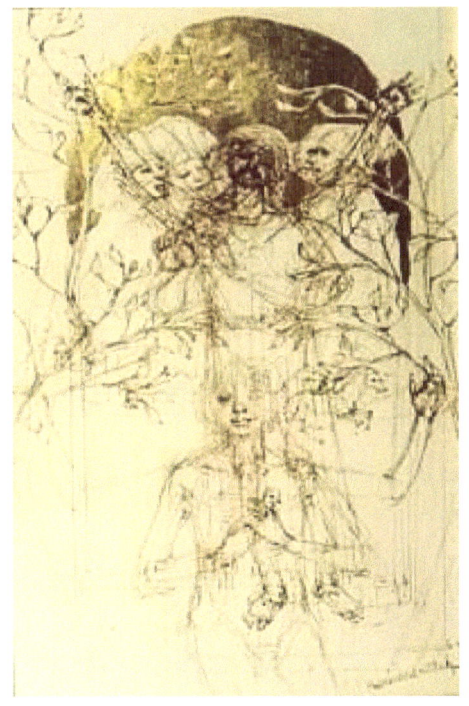

St, Francis as a Boy 1978

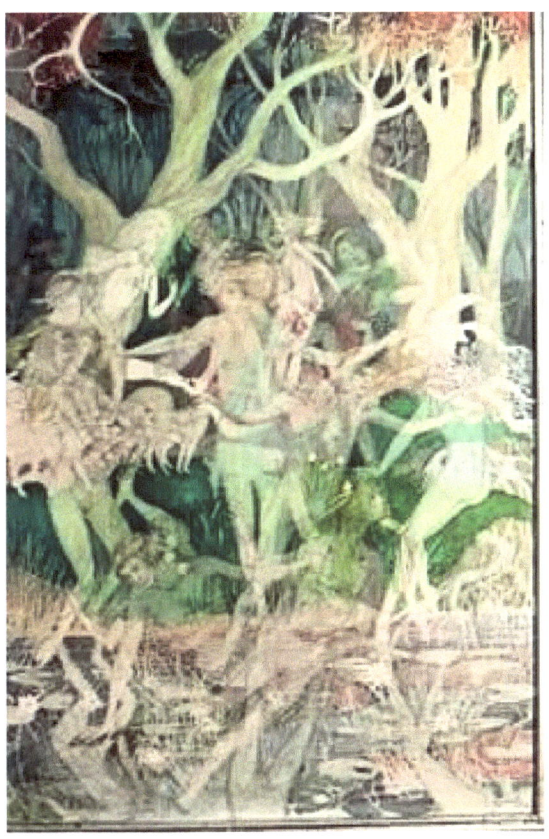

Narcissus 1965

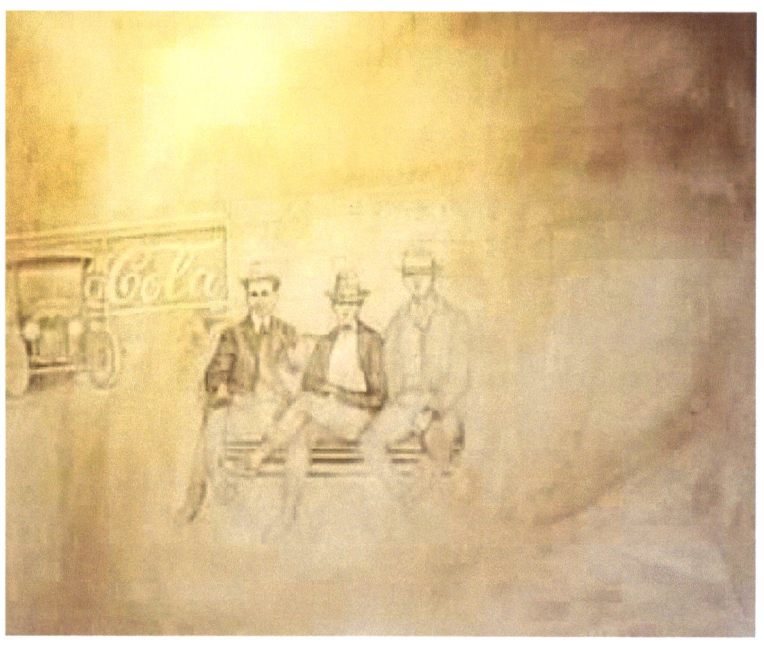

Uncle Mike and the Dollar Boys 1983

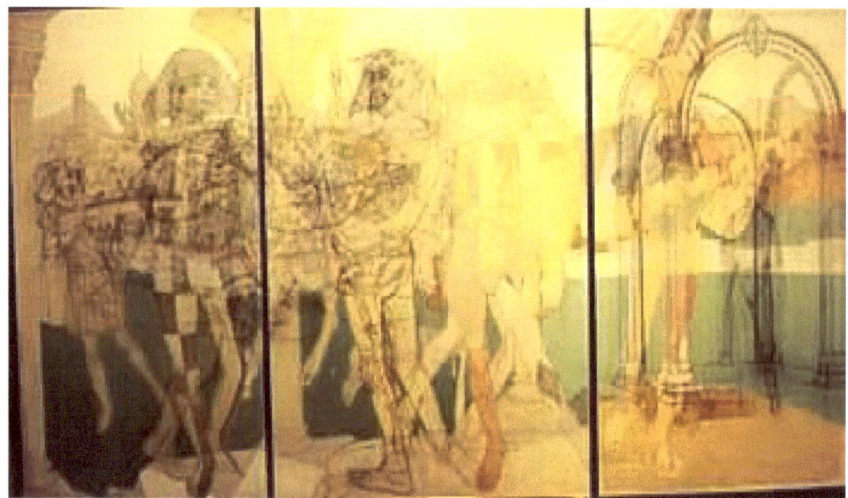

Harlequin With One Blue Eye 1975

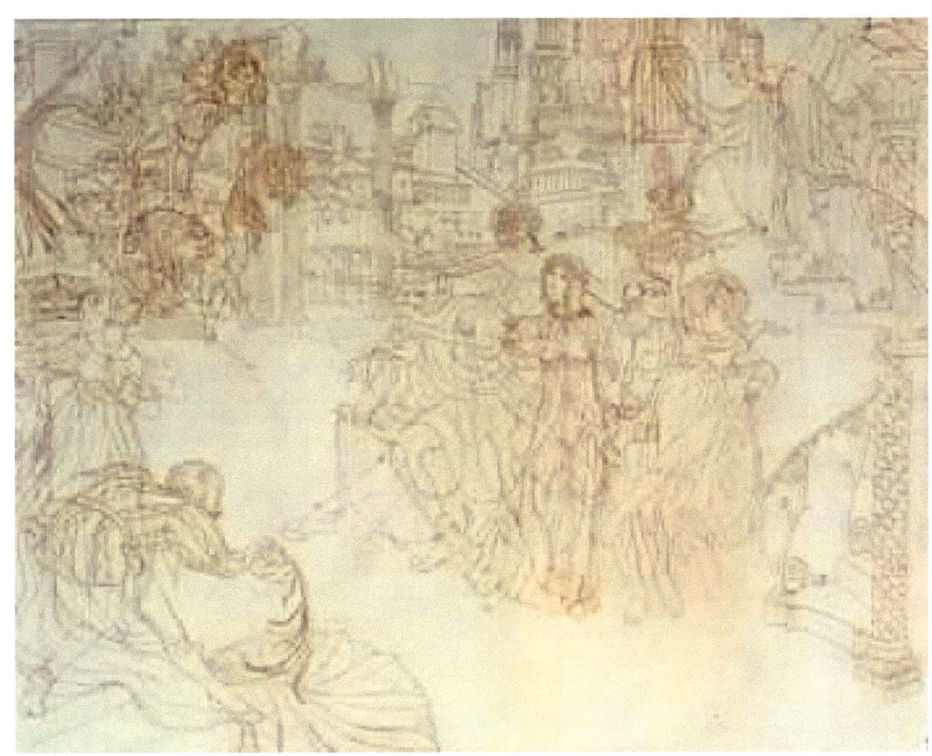

Til Eulespiegel 1980

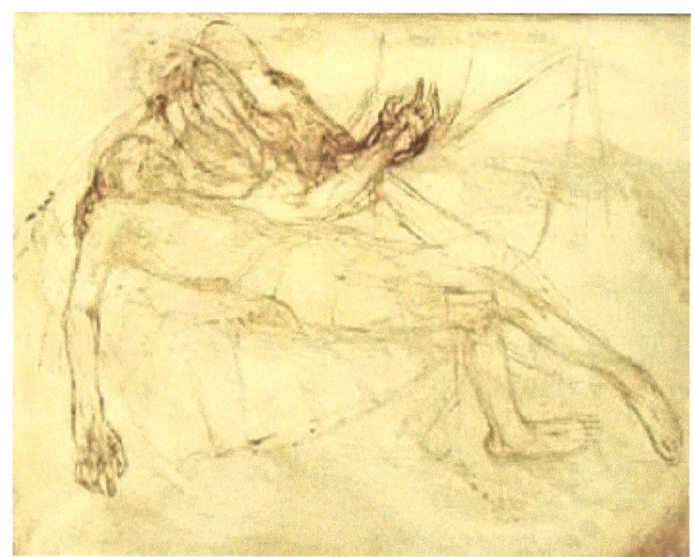

Pieta 1961

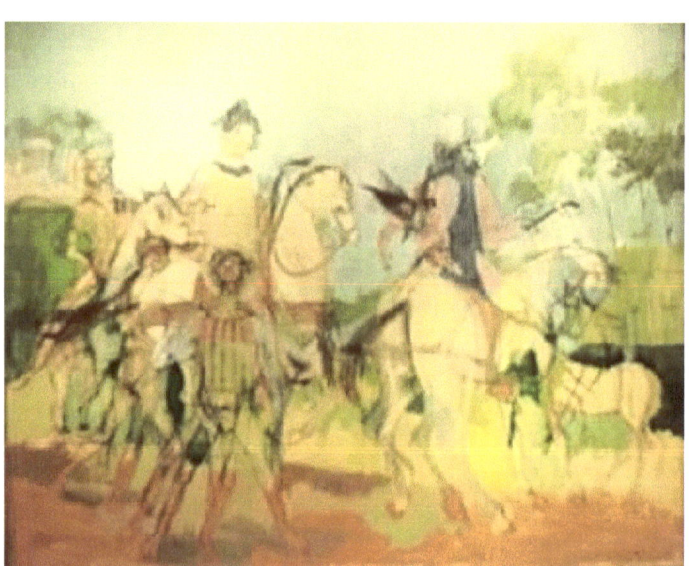

Horsemen of Manuta 1967

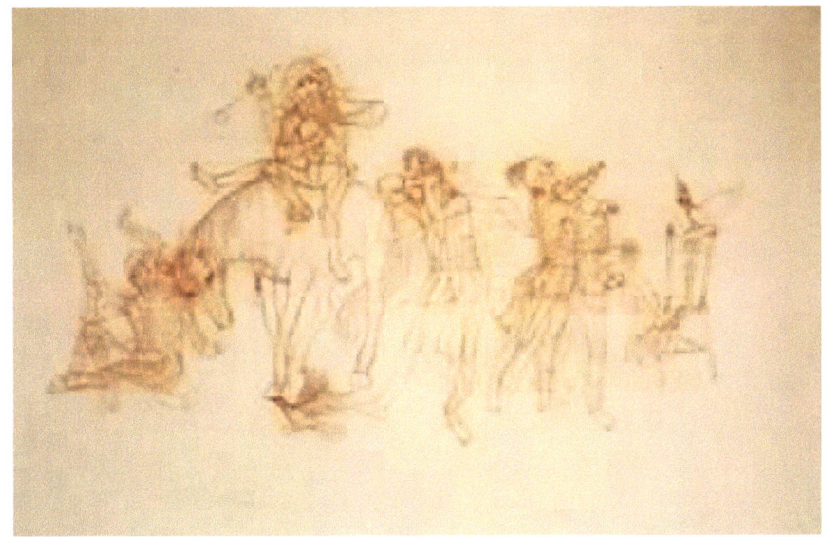

The Harlequins 1974

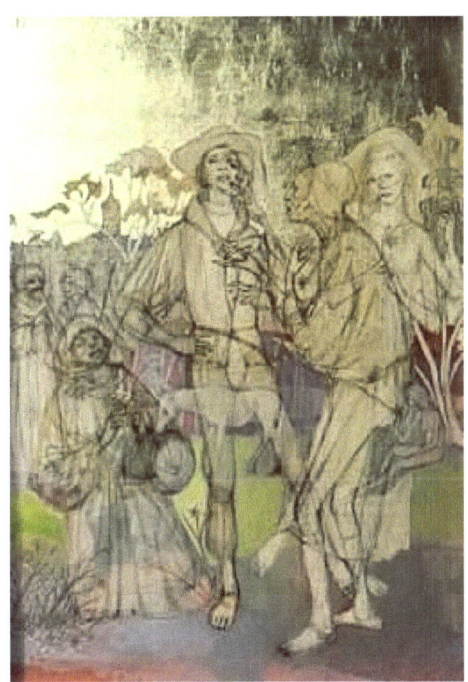

Harlequin Reciting a Nursey Rhyme 1970

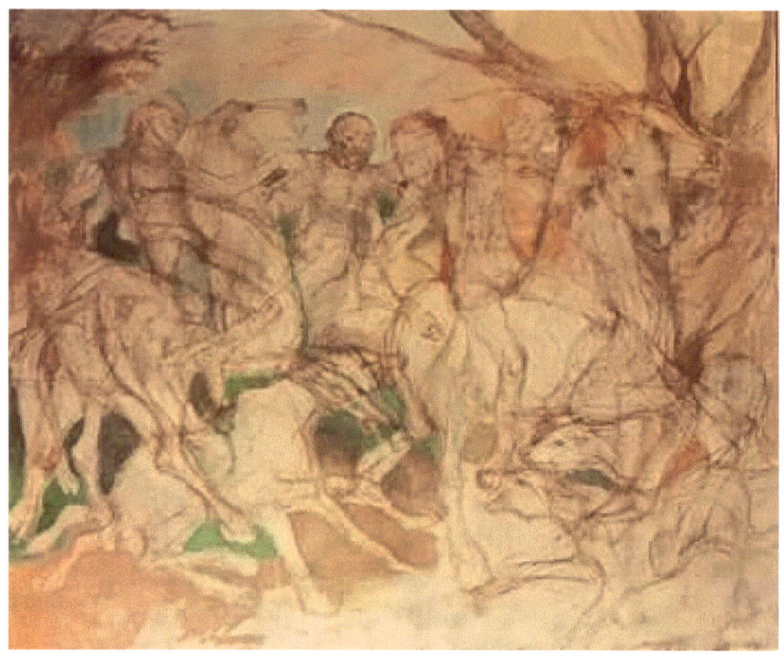

Wolf Hunt 1965

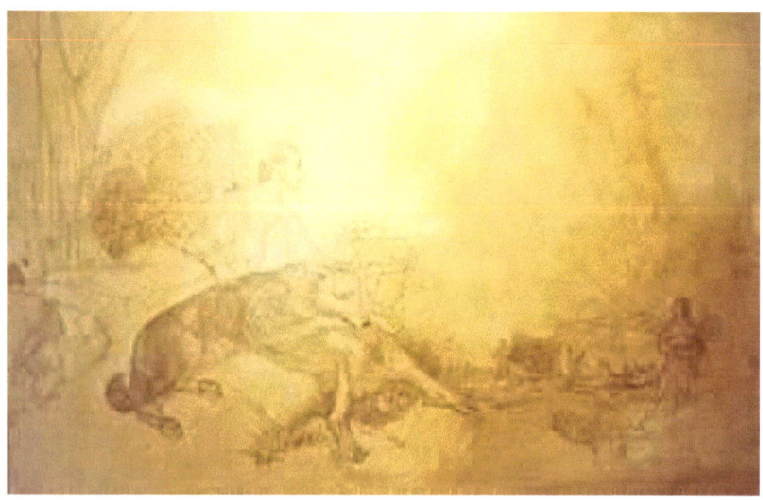

Hill Overlooking Gubio 1983

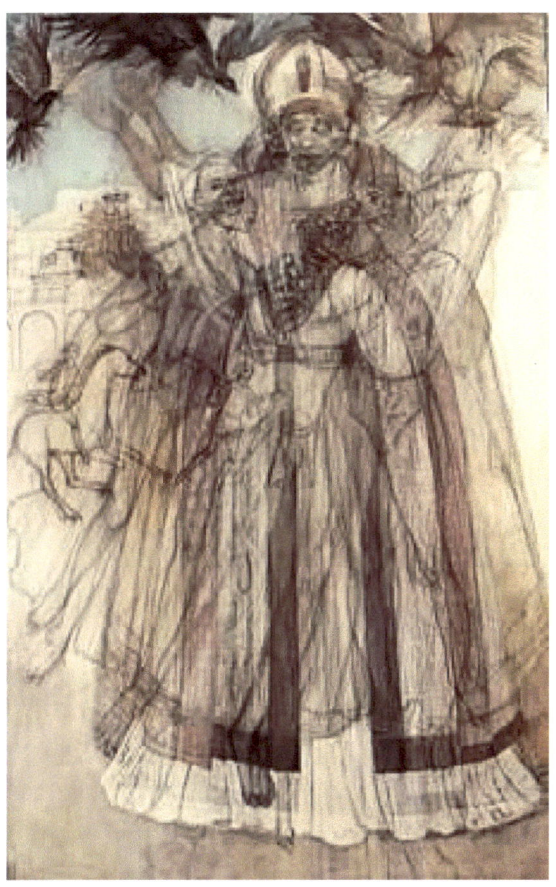

Four and Twenty Blackbirds 1980

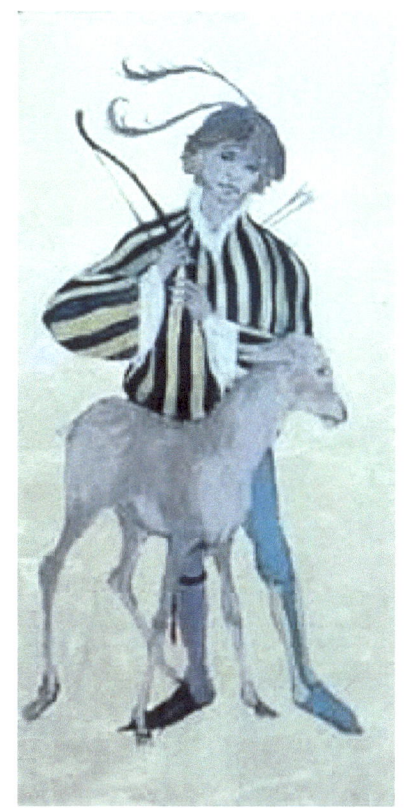

St. Giles and the wounded fawn 1960

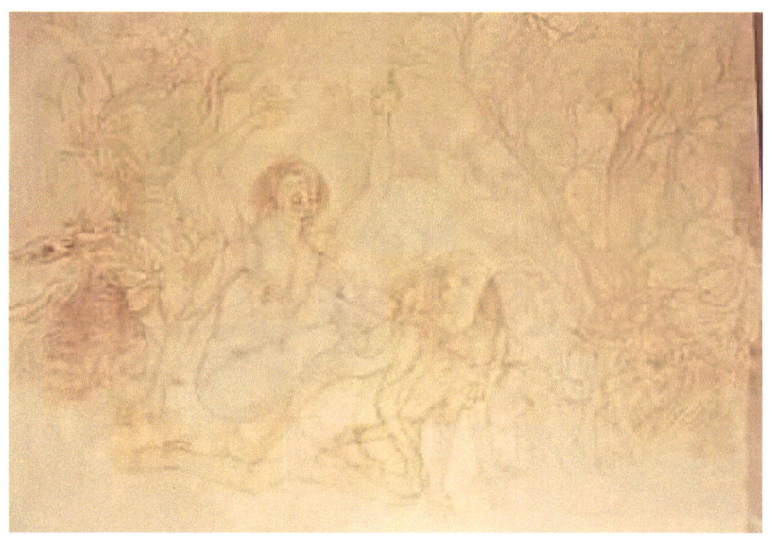

The Garden of Eden 1980

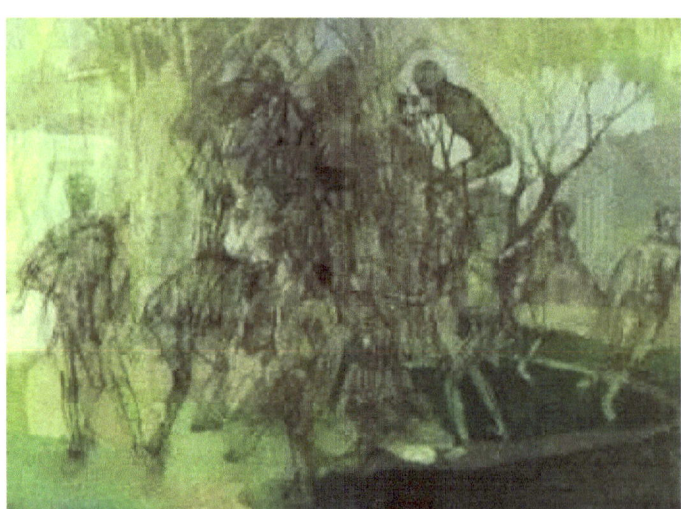

Temple in the Park 1972

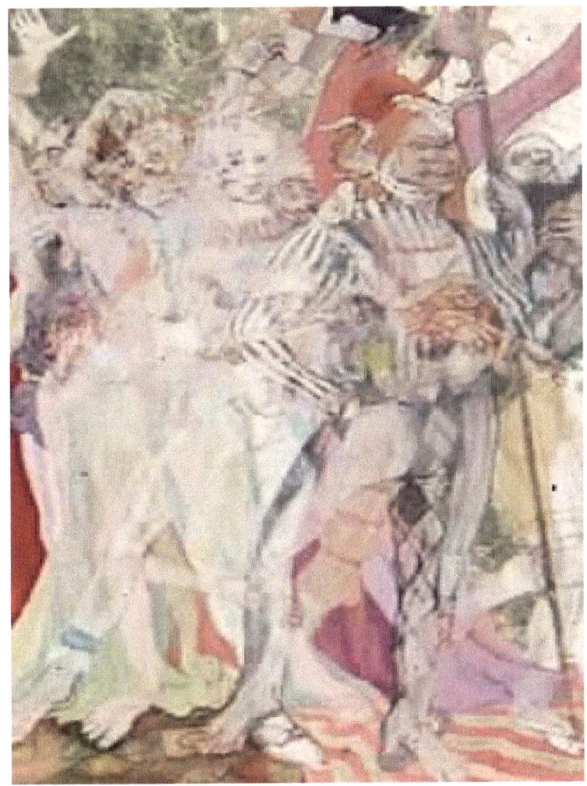

The Players 1962

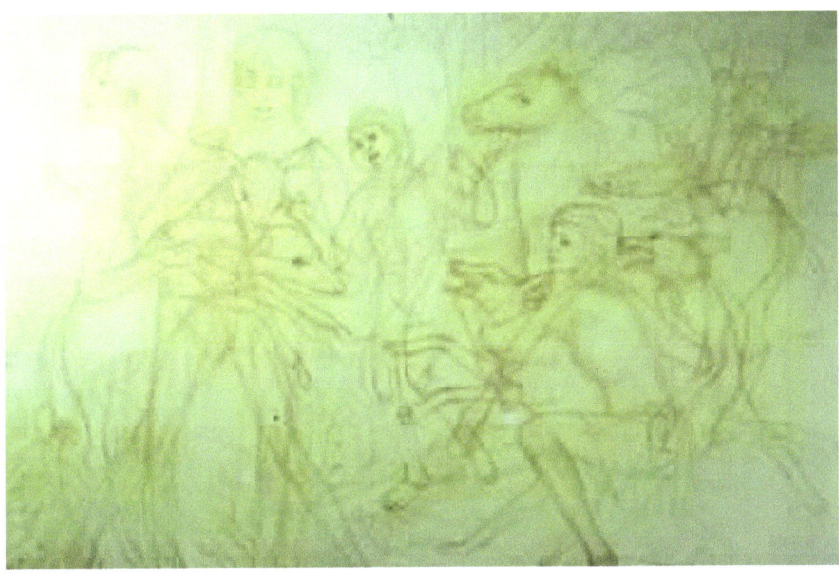

The Hunt 1974

Battle of Anghiari (after Leonardo da Vinci) 1960

Bernard Riley was always interested in art of the Renaissance. He was particularly fascinated by DaVincis Battle of Anghirari. He did several paintings and a woodcut print based on the work. The painting was in the collection of the Metropolitan Museum in New York City

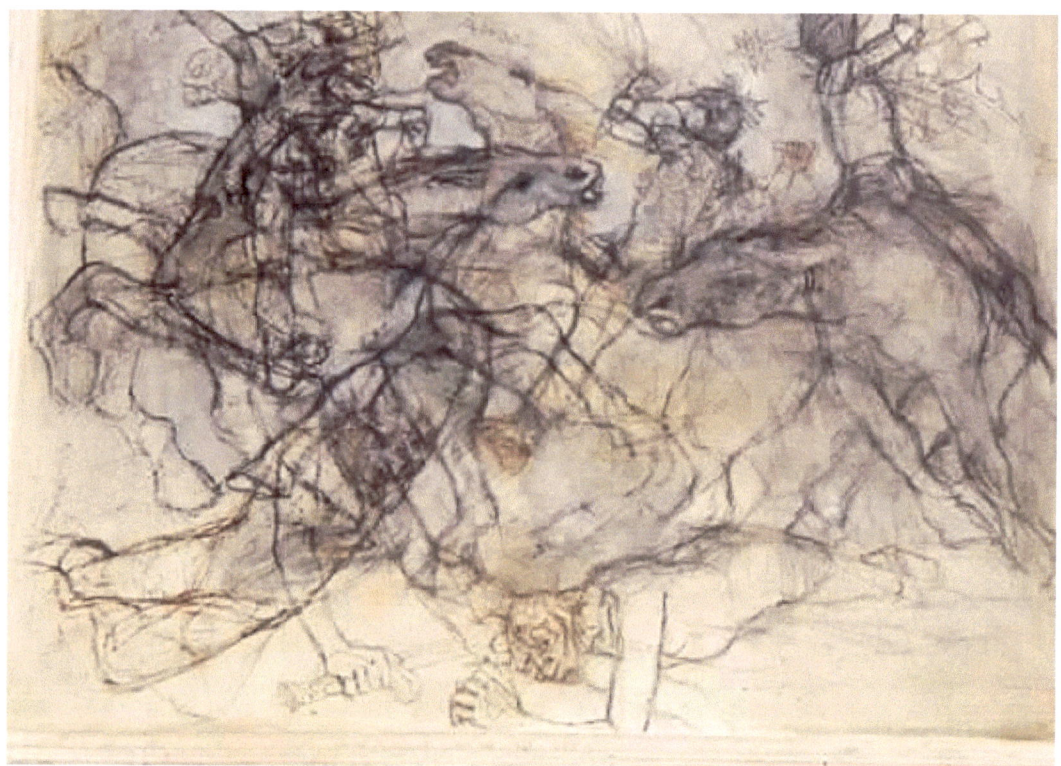

The Battle of Angerhi details

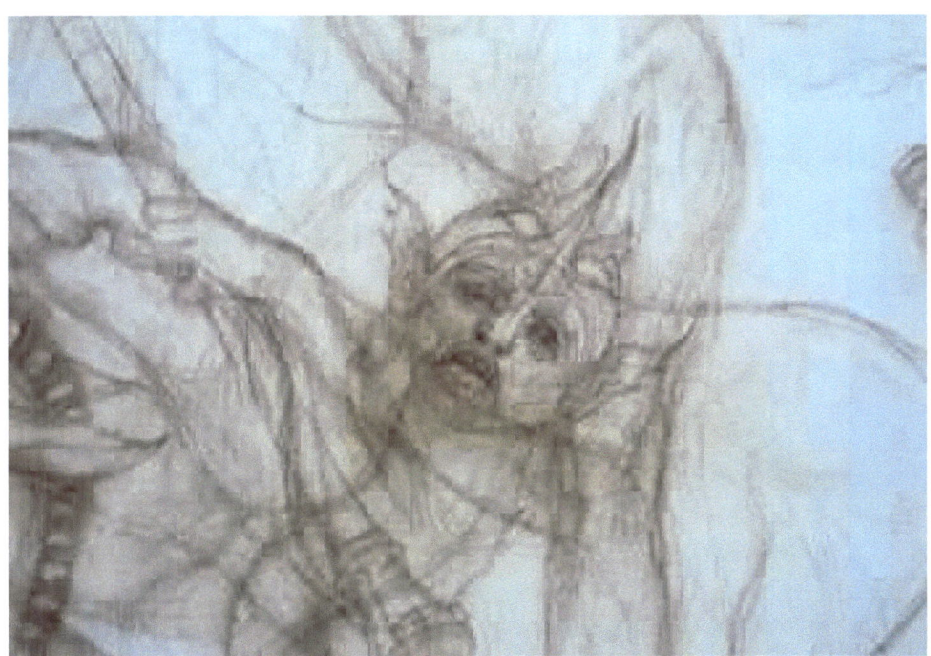

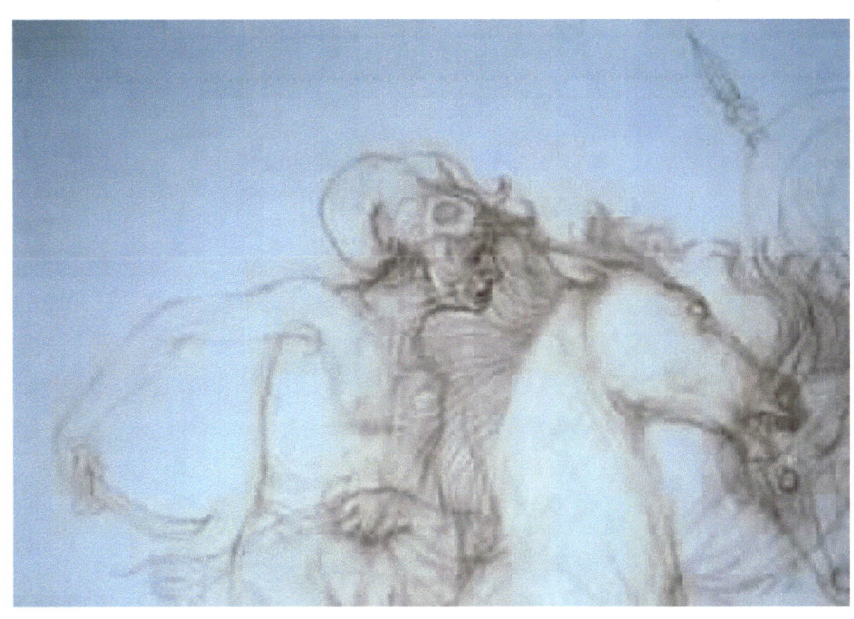

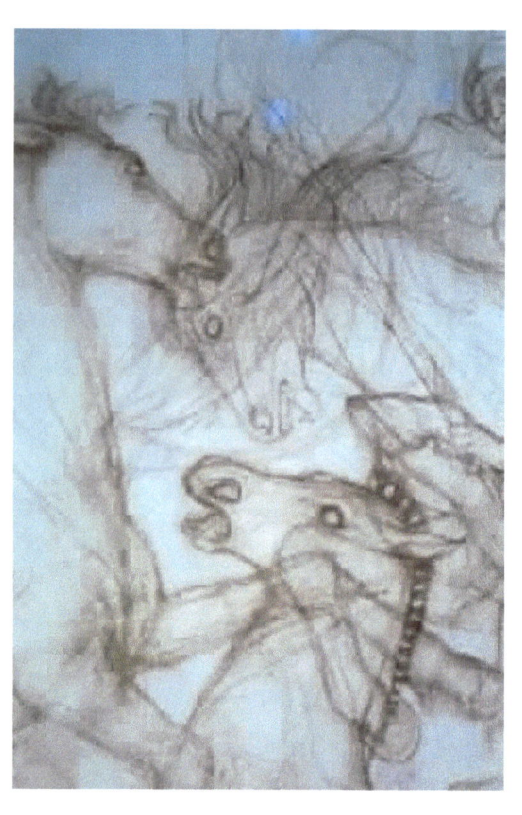
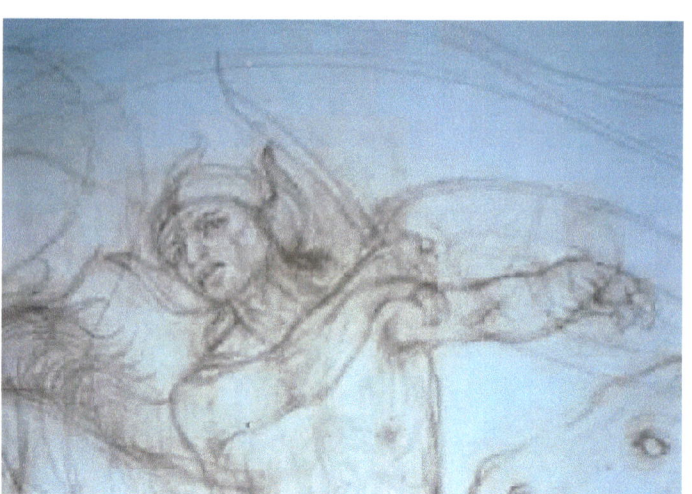
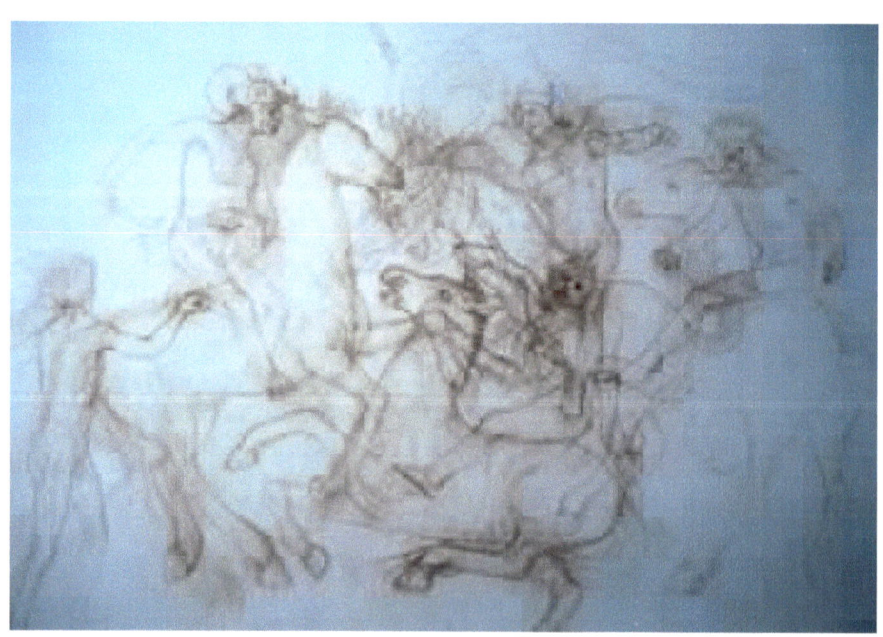

Etchings, sketches and drawings

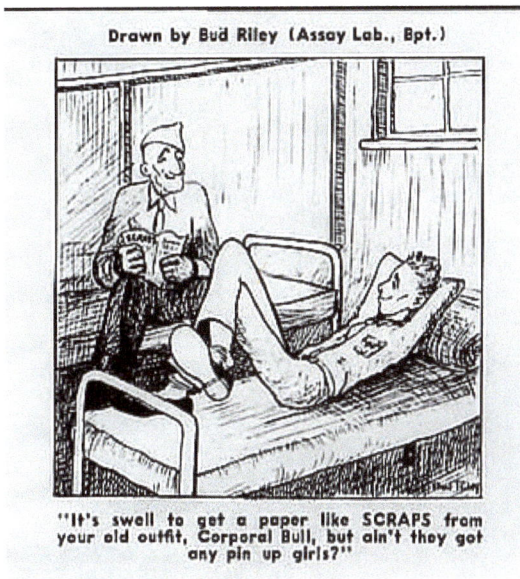

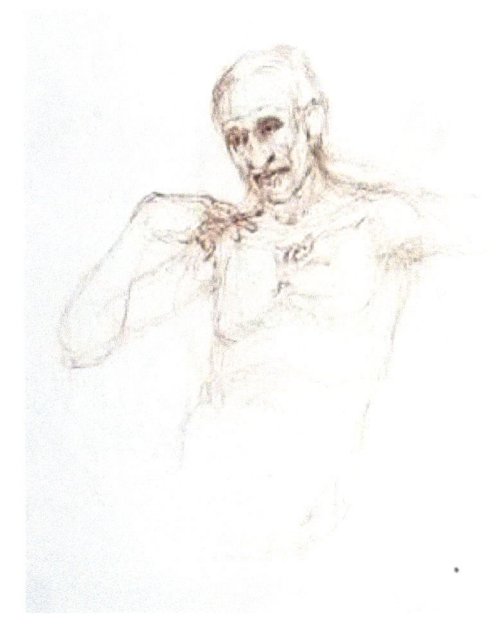

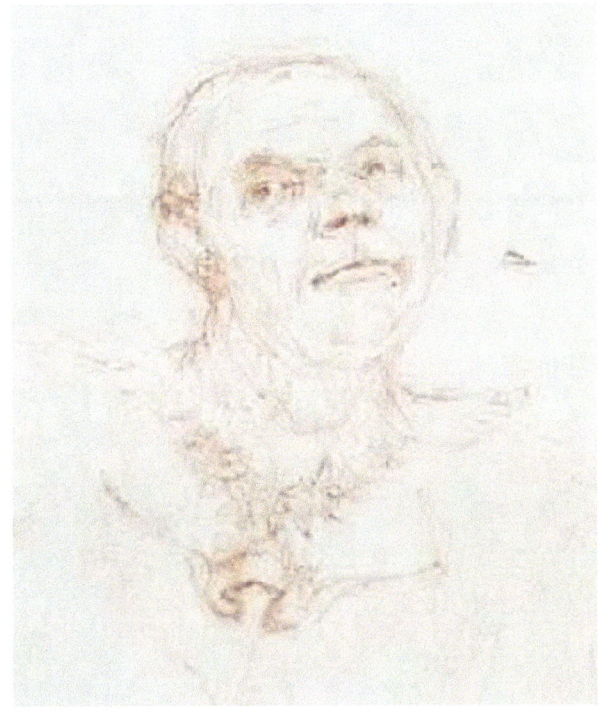

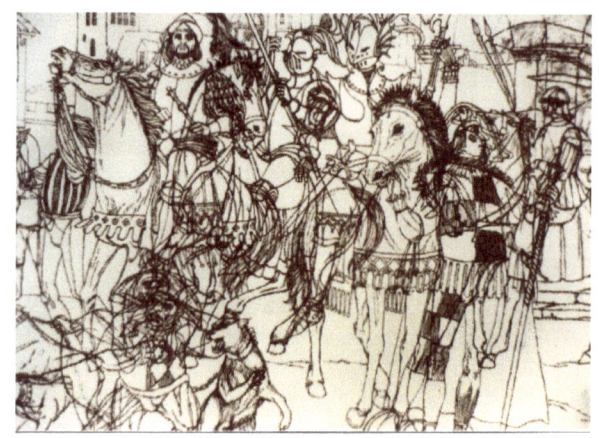

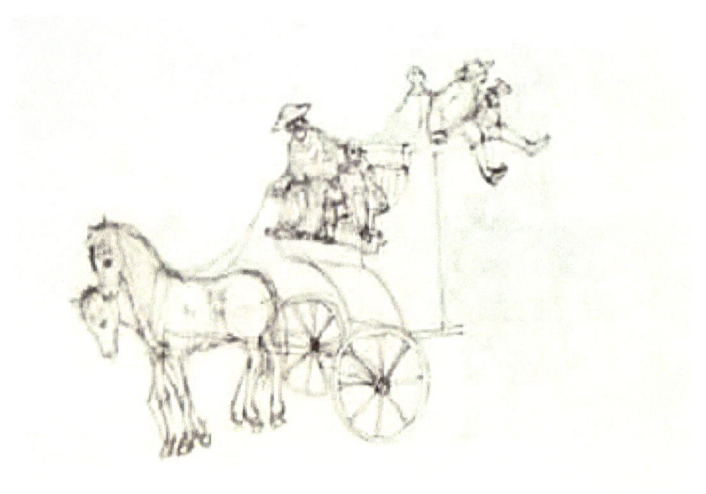

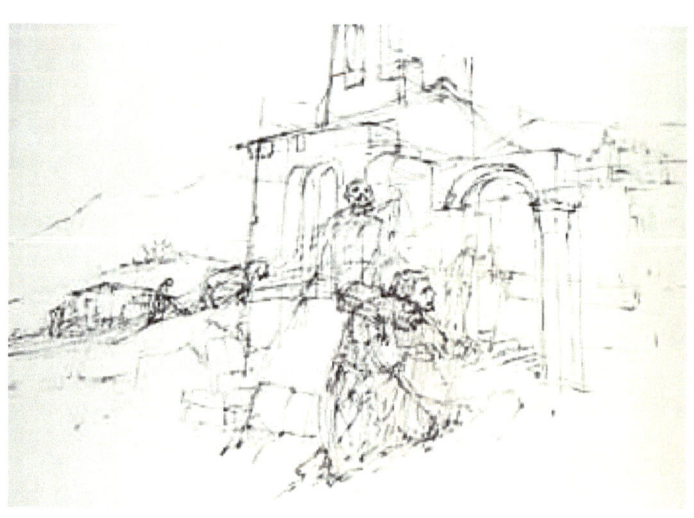

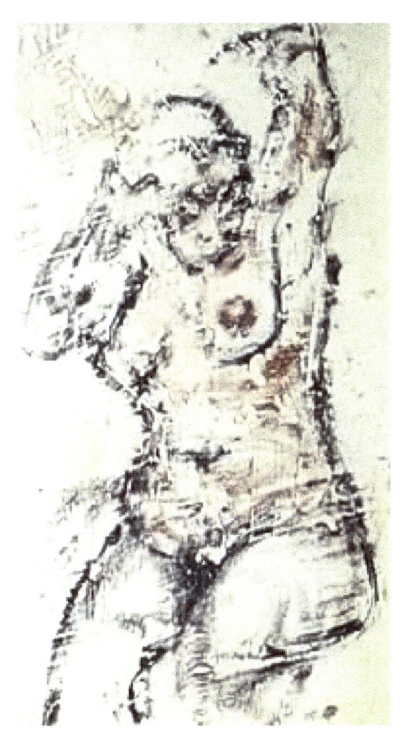
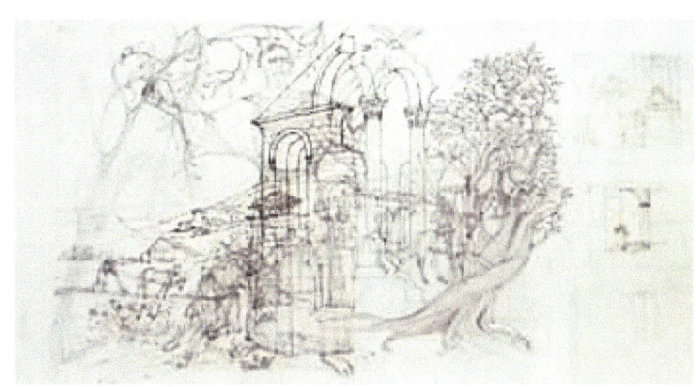
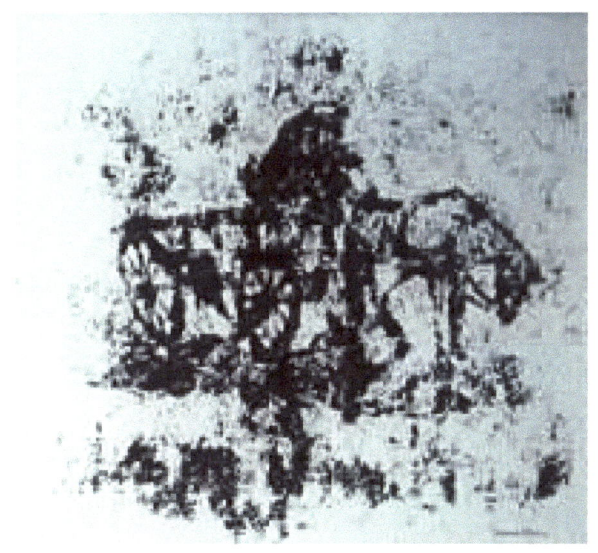

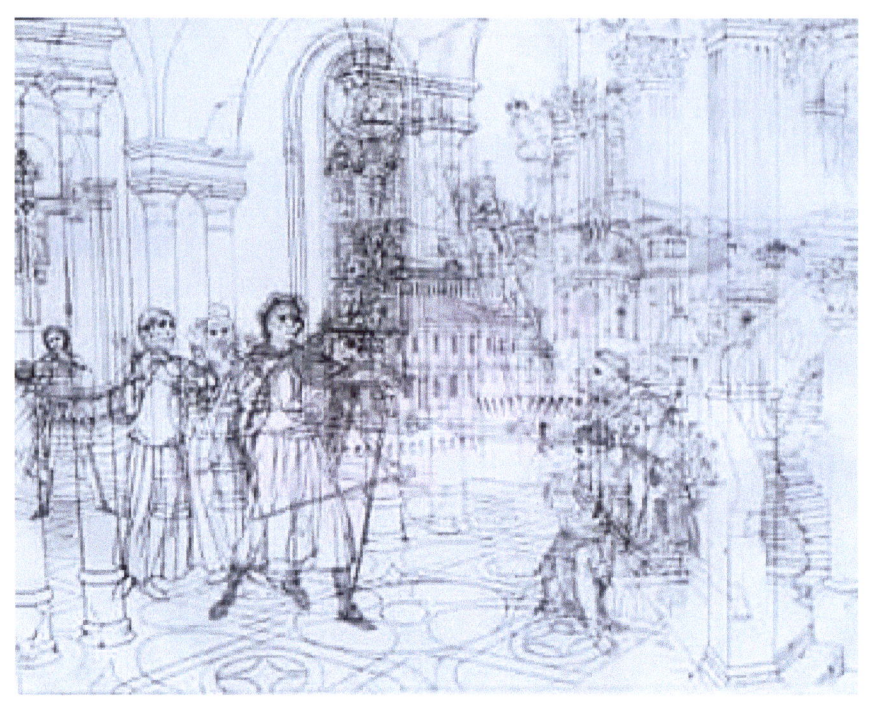

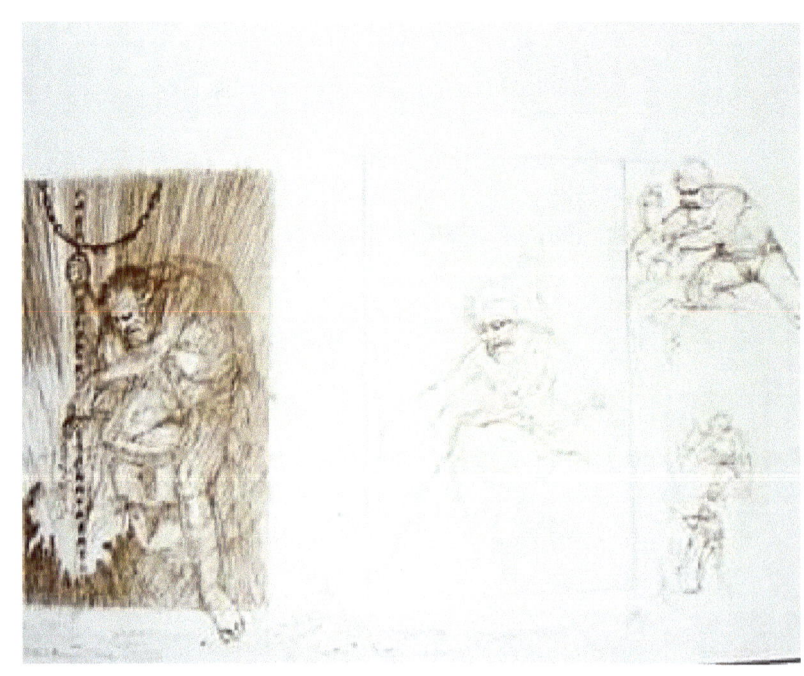

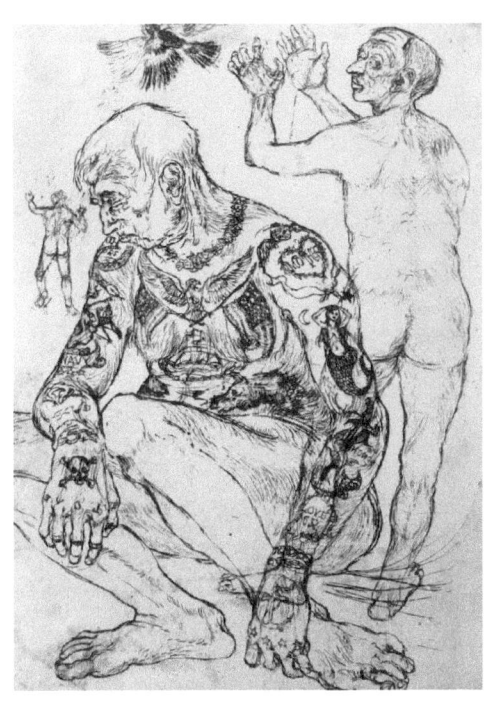
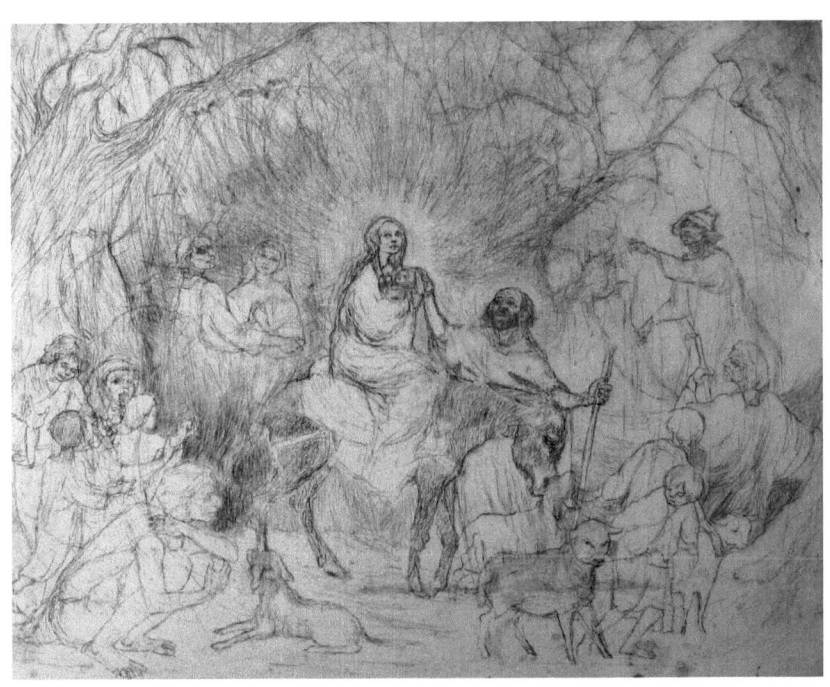

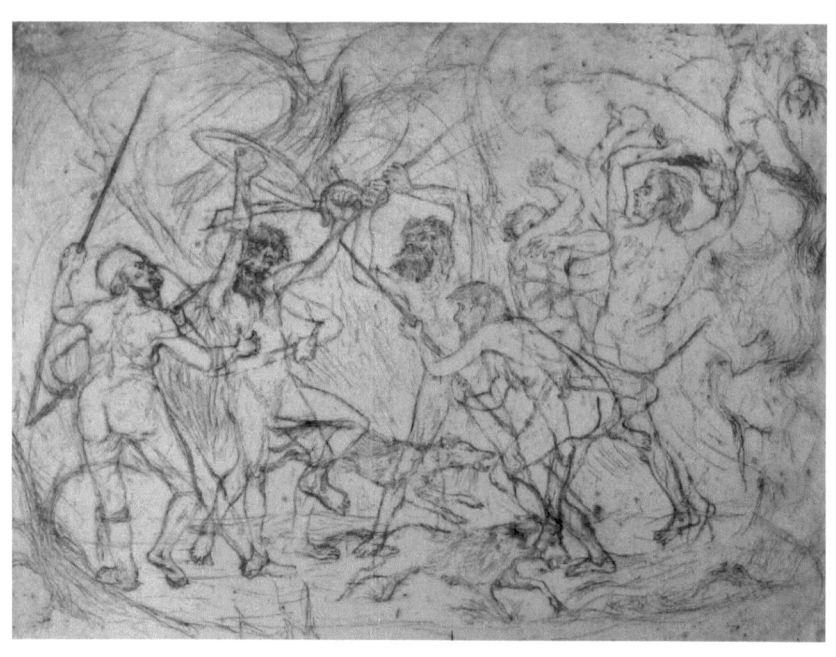

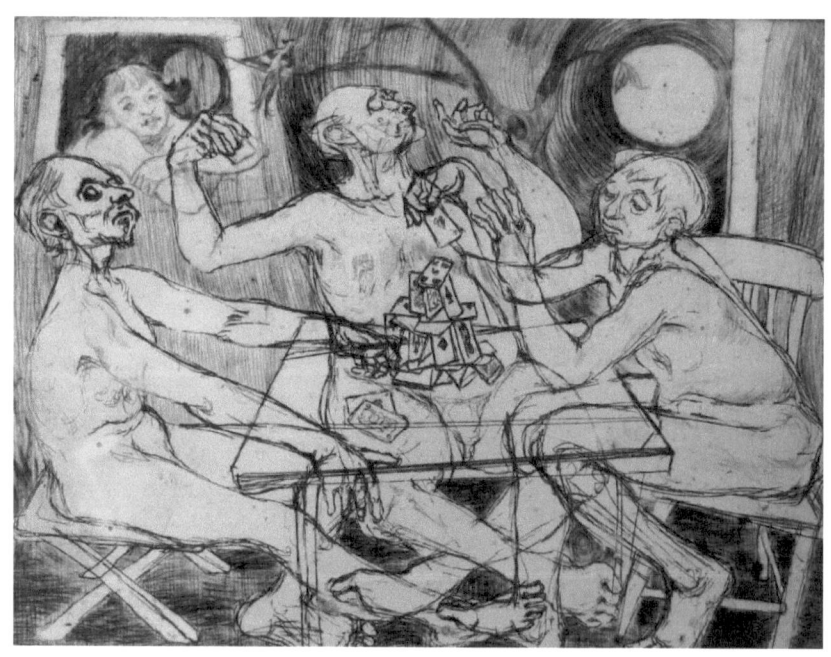

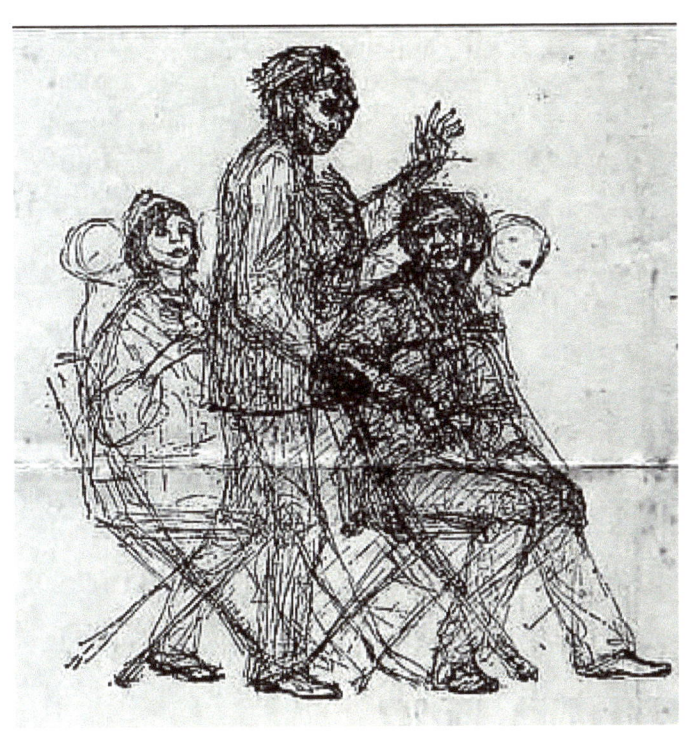
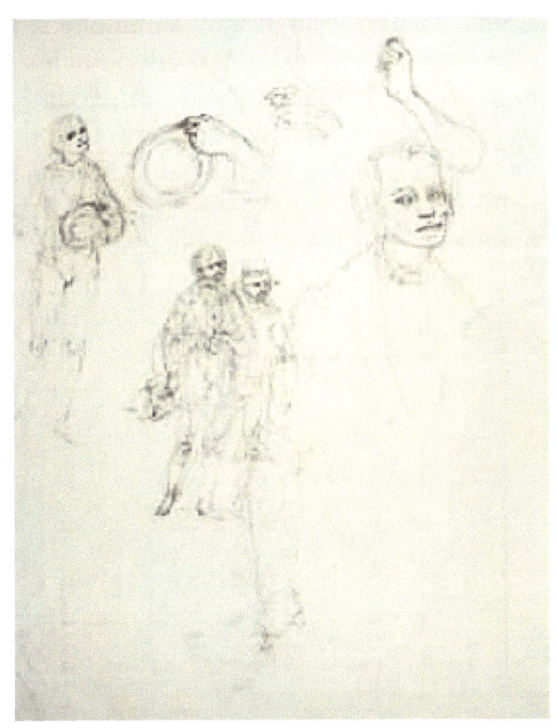
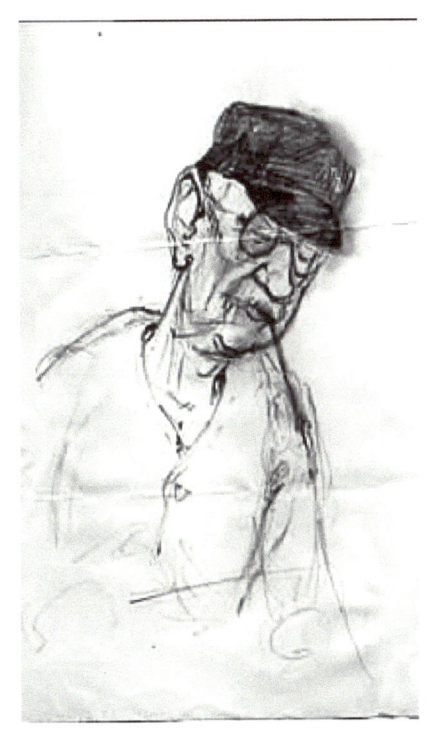

Religious Works

Bernard Riley was raised in a Catholic family and maintained that faith throughout his life. He created a series of Life of the Saints works; small single portraits, with many done with gold leaf background. The urge to paint on a grand scale was fulfilled in 1959 when he designed a detailed narrative mural recording the life of St. Aloysius Gonzaga for Fairfield University. "Aloysius was a very severe type of person. He was very, very dedicated. He was a wealthy man, came from very powerful people. The Gonzagas were, this is back in the Fourteenth Century, they were strong, powerful people. They had the power of life and death over hundreds of serfs and the people that lived on the land and worked the land for them. Aloysius just threw it over, just like Saint Francis, just threw the whole thing over, and went to join the Jesuits."

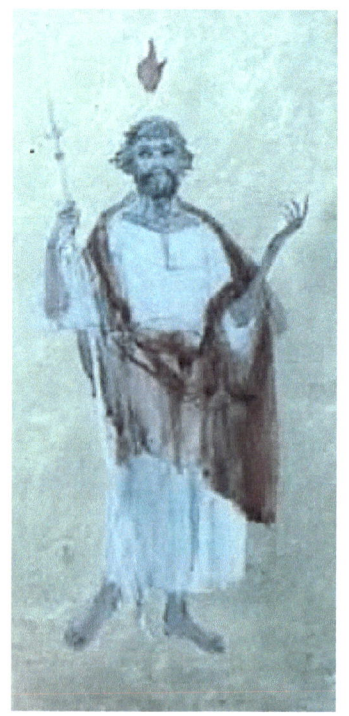

St. Jude

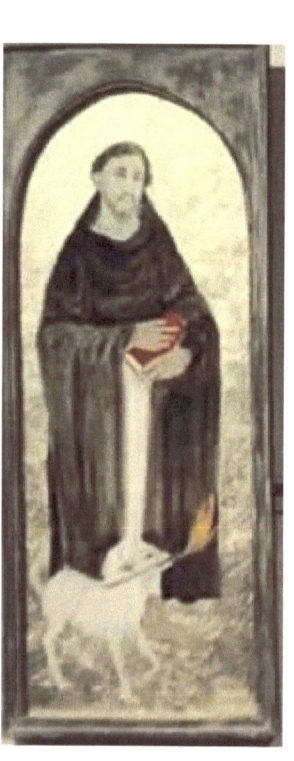

St. Dominic

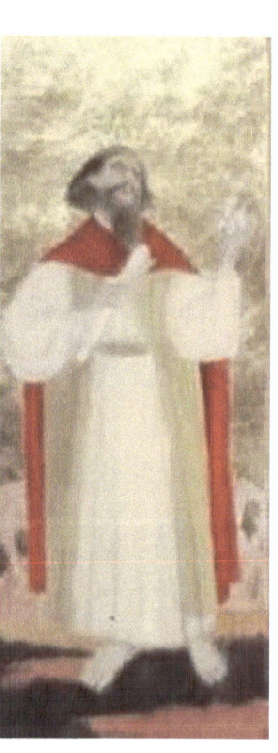

St. John the Baptist

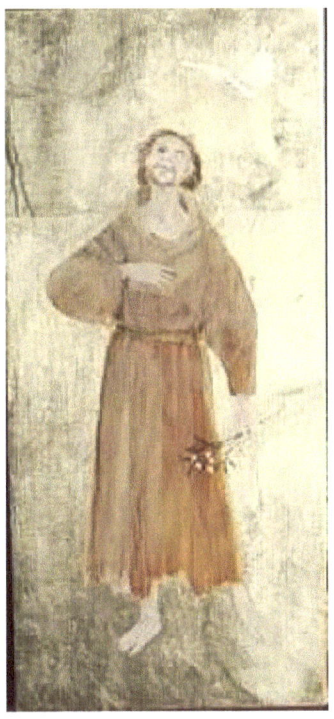

St. Francis

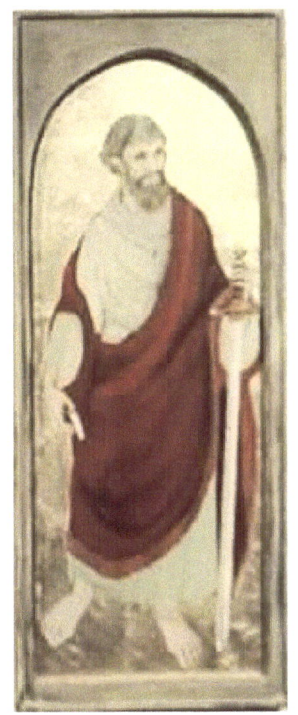

St. Paul

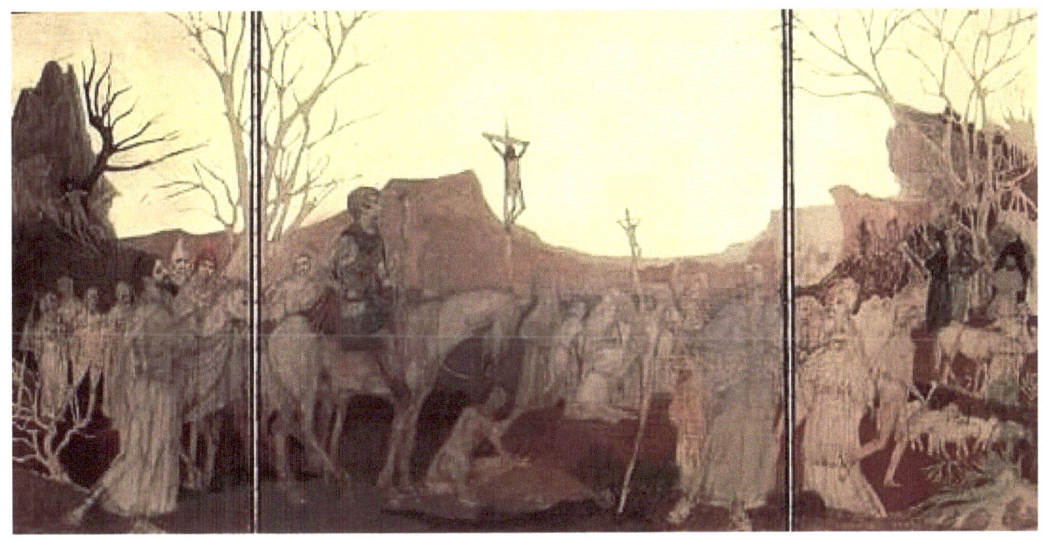

The Crucifixion

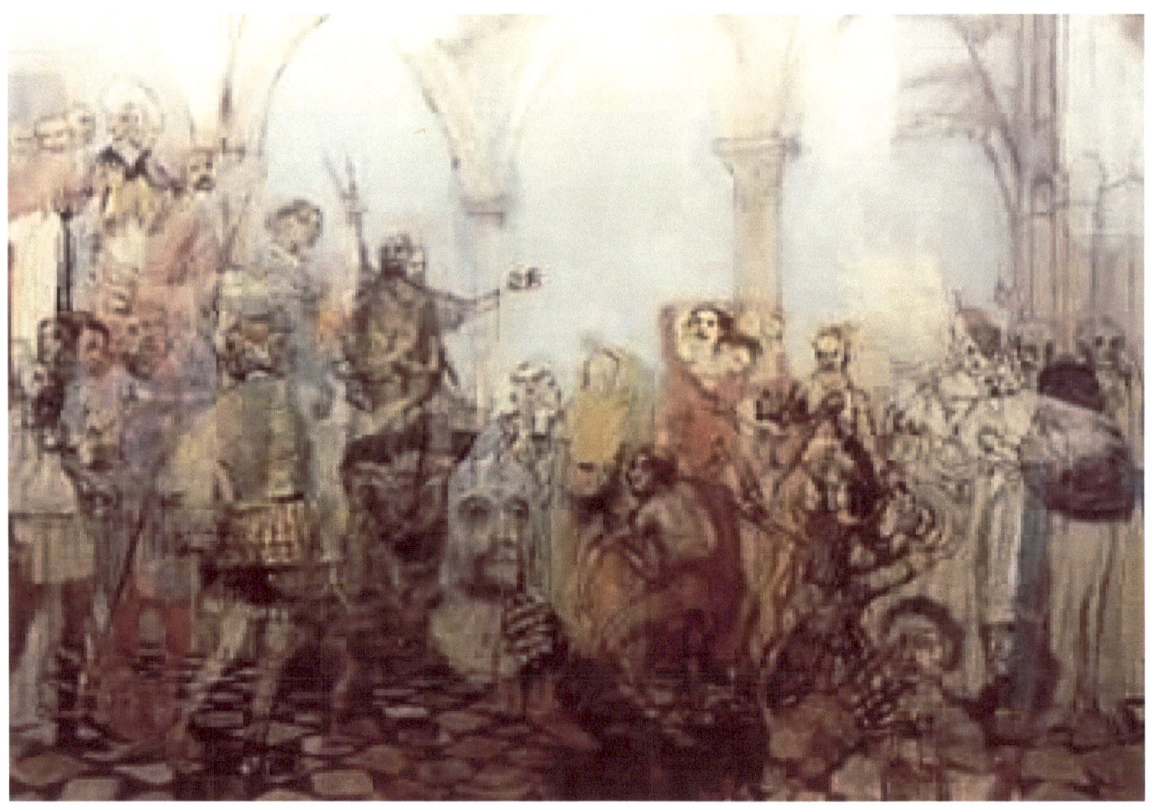

St, Francis and the Woman Possessed by the Devil

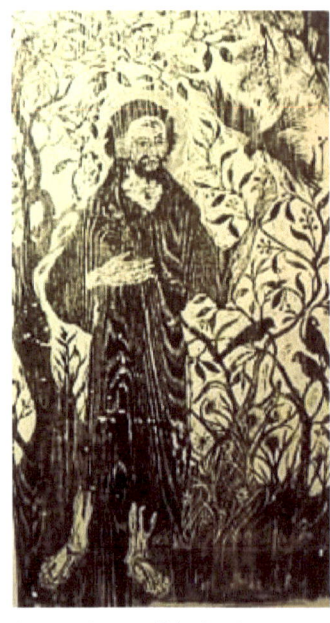

St Francis woodblock print

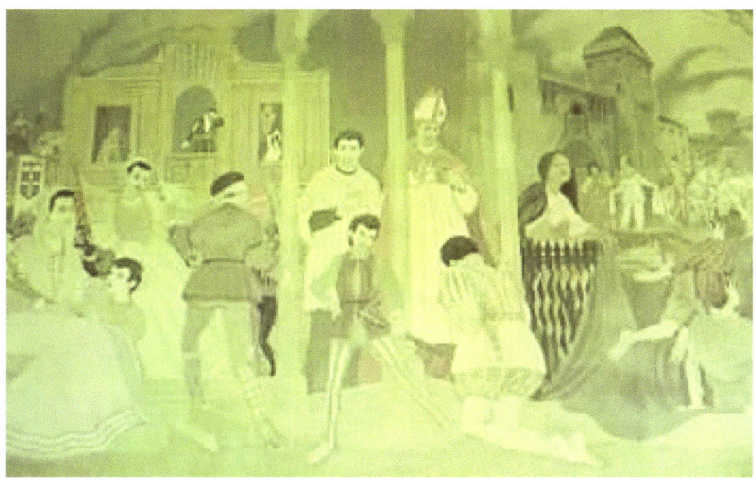

Mural in Gonzaga Hall

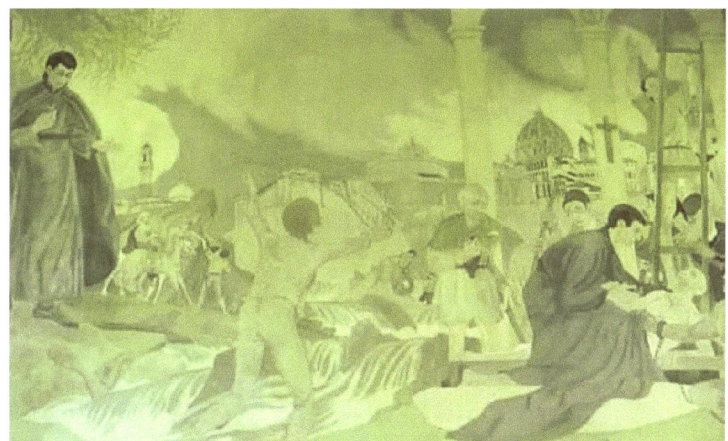

Fairfield University 1959

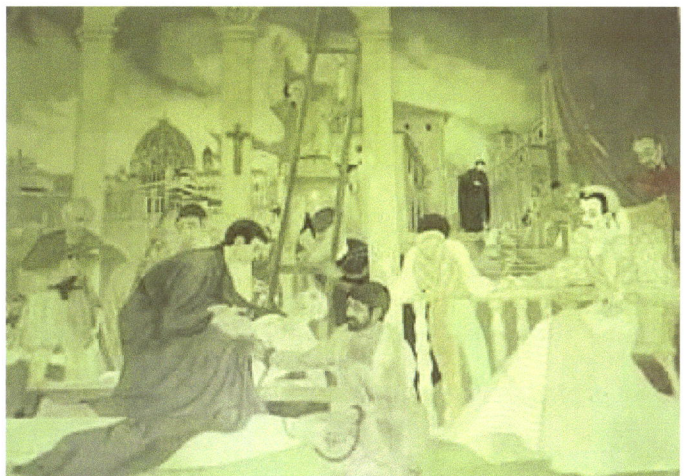

The Procession, 1968

This is 12 foot long. It was just the idea of feeling that panels made something different and the space sort of pointed in the direction of procession.

The figures moving across that space seem to have to be. This was done strictly without planning and without sketches, but done directly on the board, completed in a hurry in order to get into a one man show that I had in the Hilton Hotel. Just a pure drawing and then I began to work on it and develop it as a painting.

This is the little man that's leading the whole procession, seated on the donkey. Not quite so much of a Harlequin but his trousers sort of look that way.

The clothes were stolen and picked up one way or another, but they were originally very rich clothing and part of some noble's wardrobe probably. But they got scattered around these people.

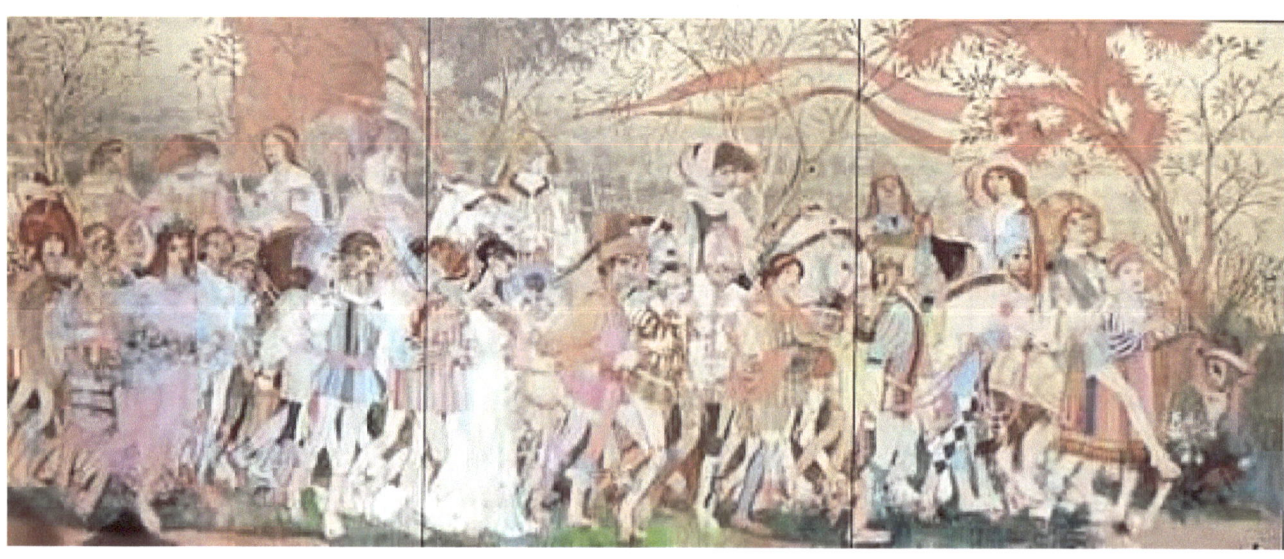

The Procession - details

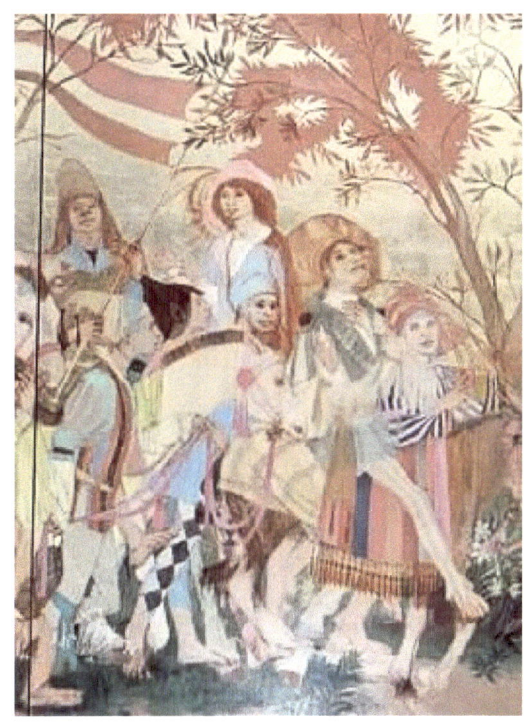

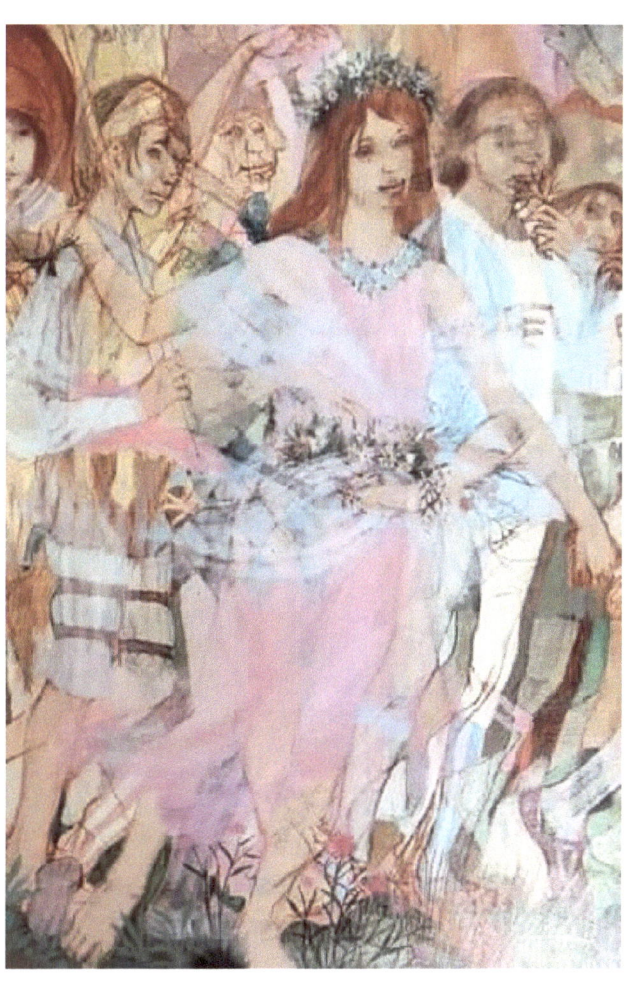

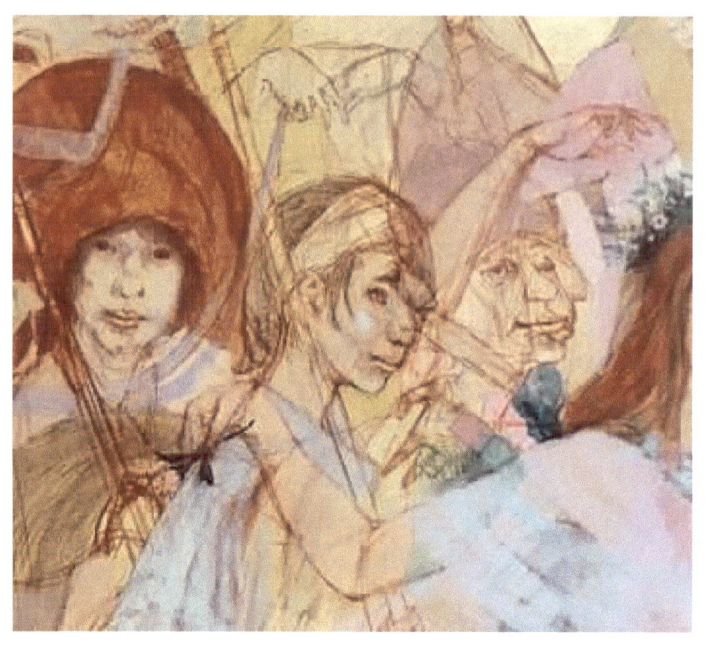

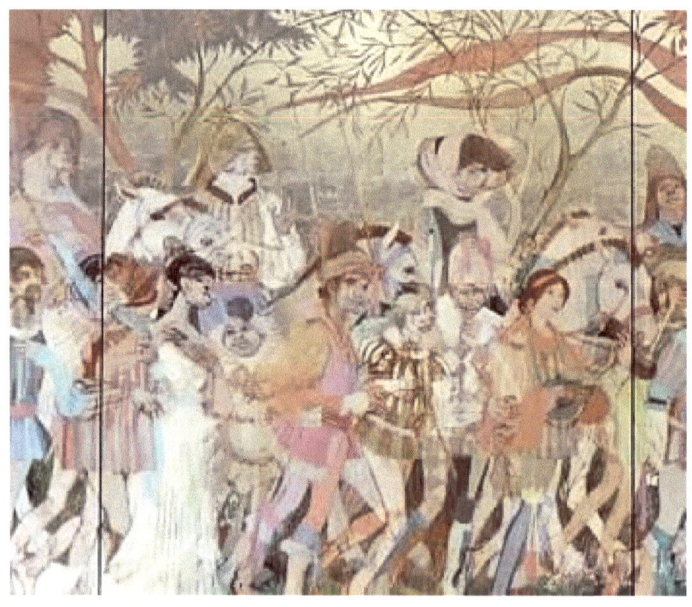

The Bird Sellers 1975

A 1975 exhibit at the Silvermine Guild of Artists featured gigantic, floor-to-ceiling drawings done with a brush. The act of drawing on a wall surface with a brush using reddish sepia is a rather outdated art technique anchored in Renaissance tradition. It becomes symbolic of the story Riley tells about the rapid disappearance of manual craftsmanship. Its bringing something new into an era that people have lost understanding of, to see someone actually doing a craft operation. They are seeing someone drawing on a wall, they wonder what can this be?

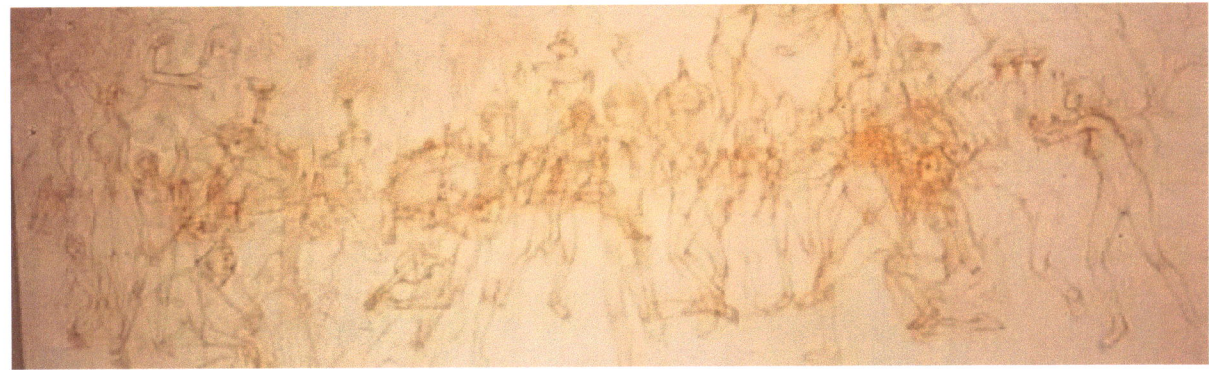

The Bird Sellers - left panel

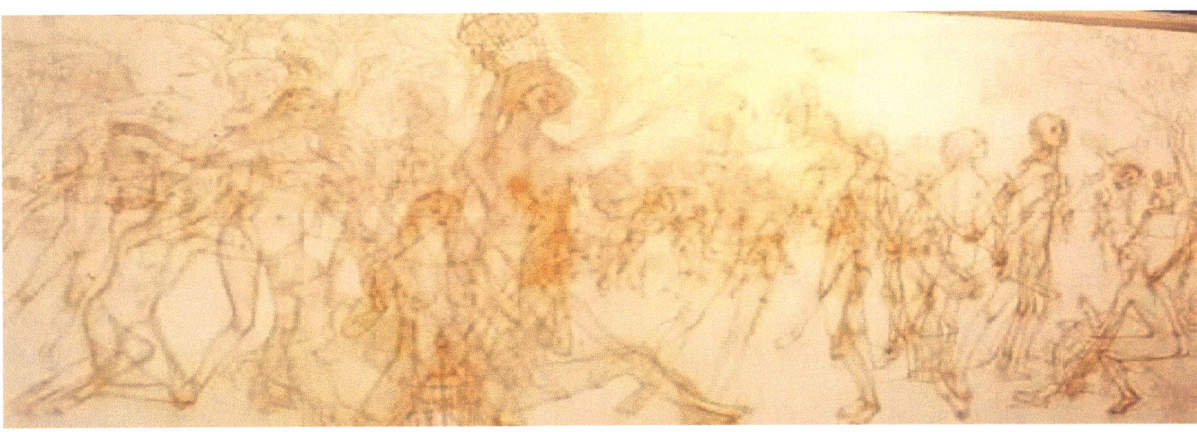

The Bird Sellers - right panel

The Bird Sellers - details

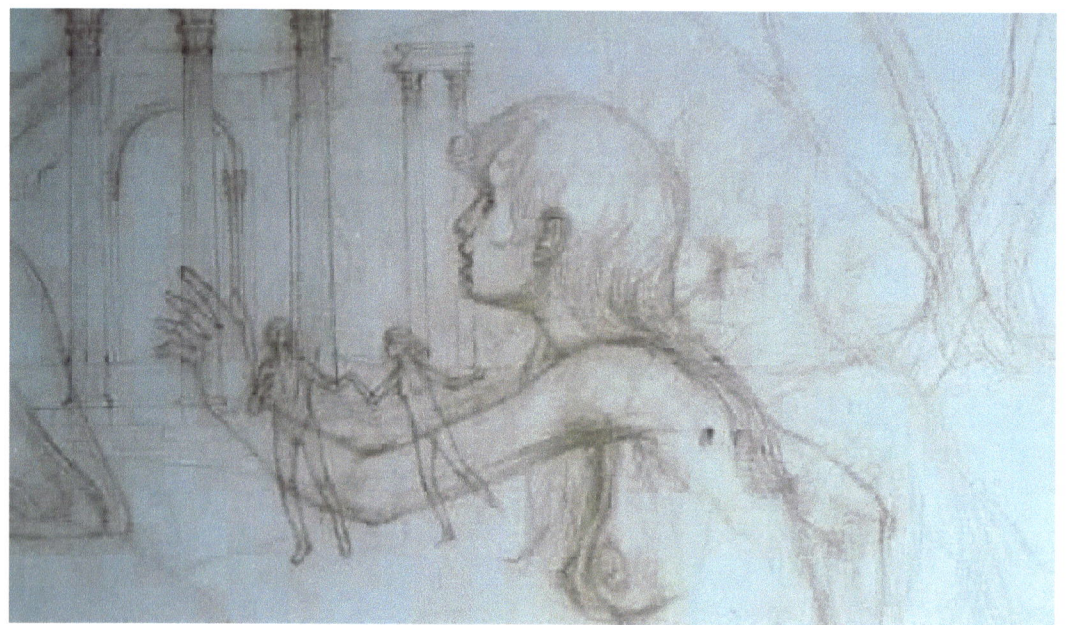

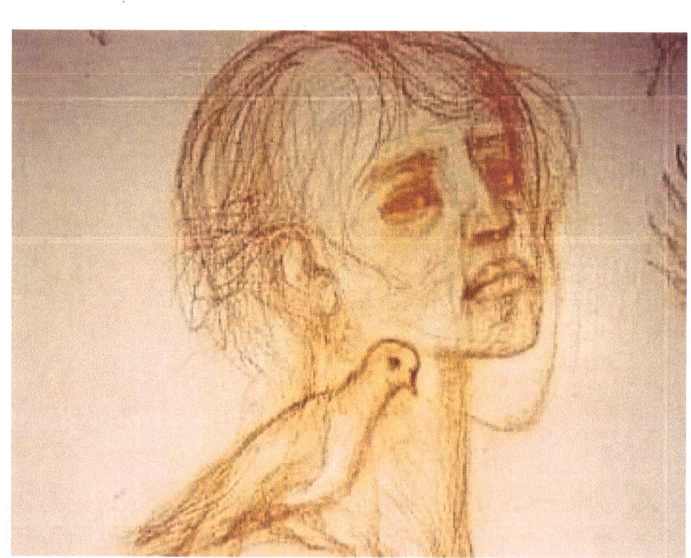

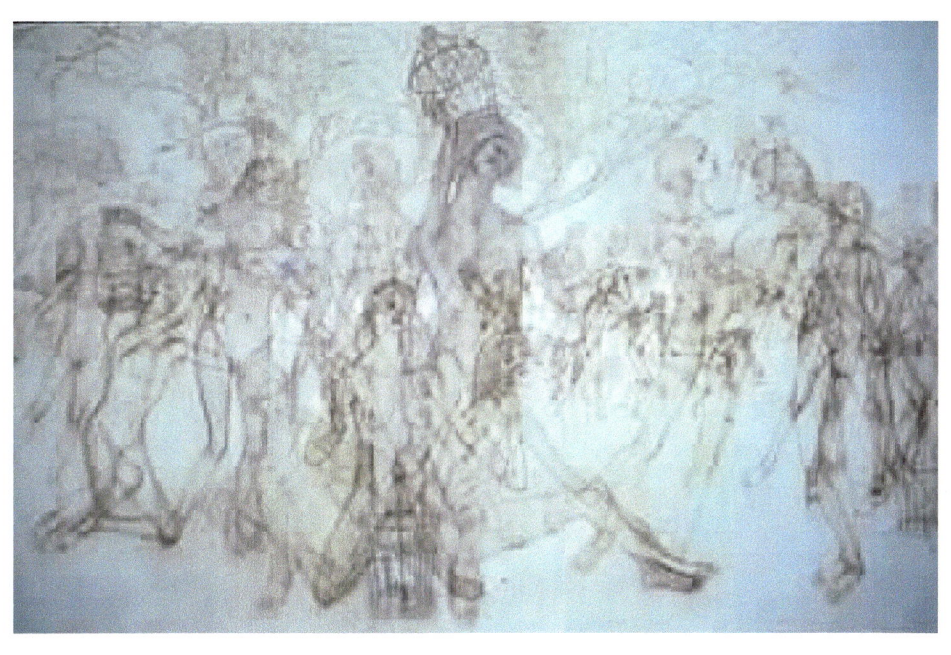

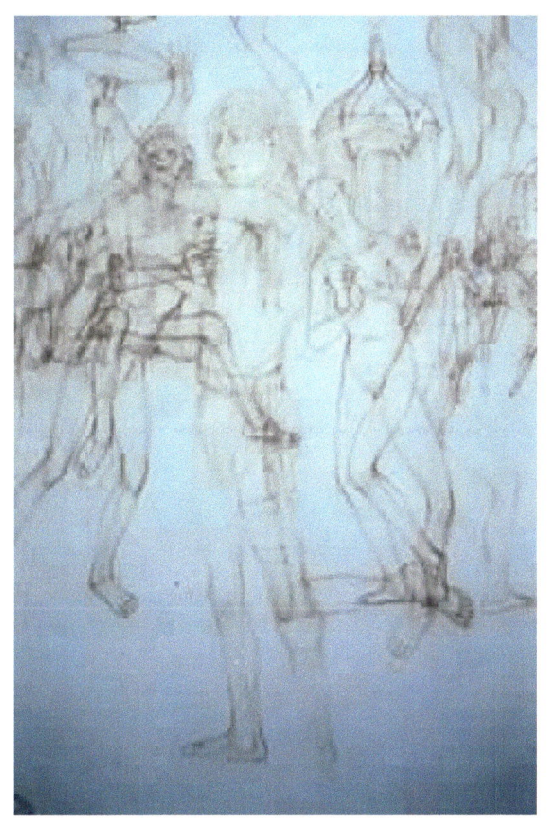

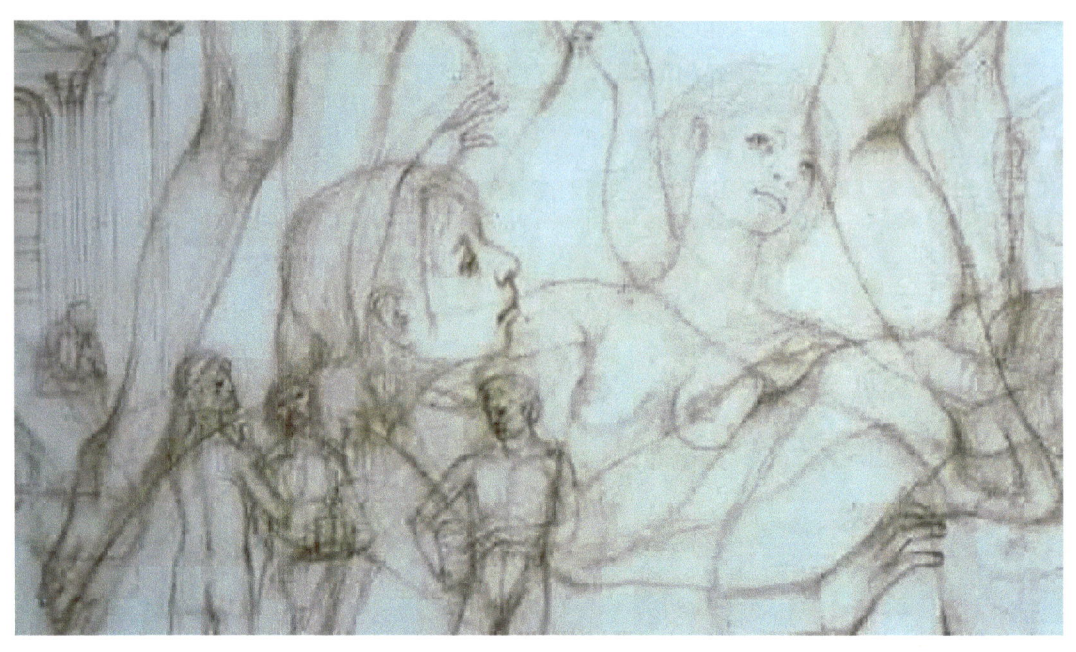
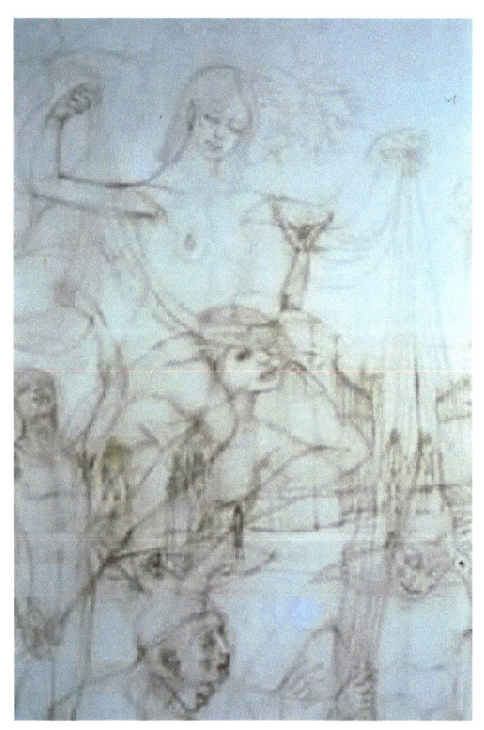

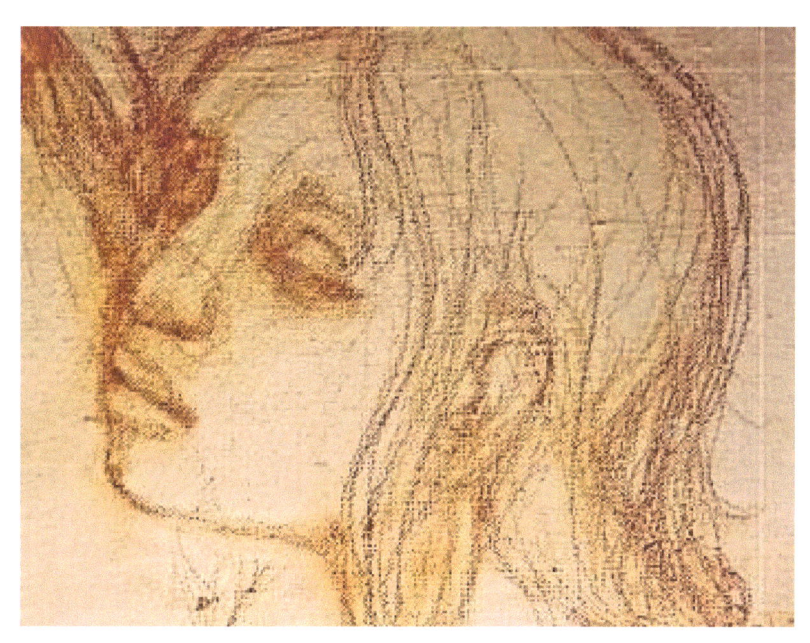

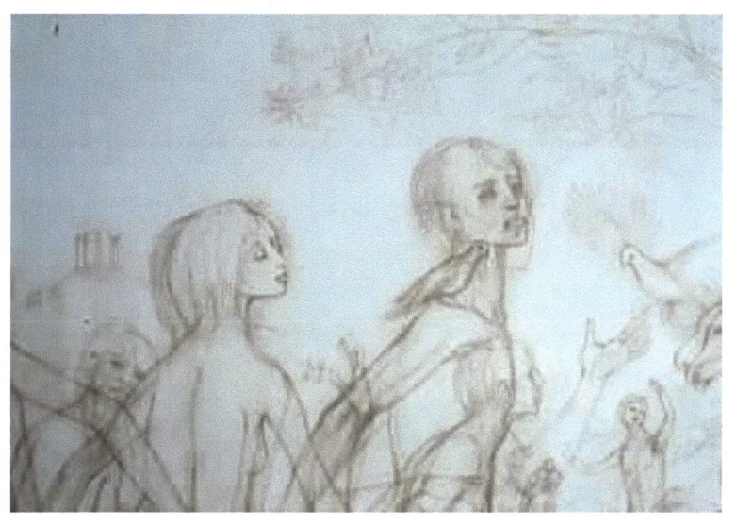

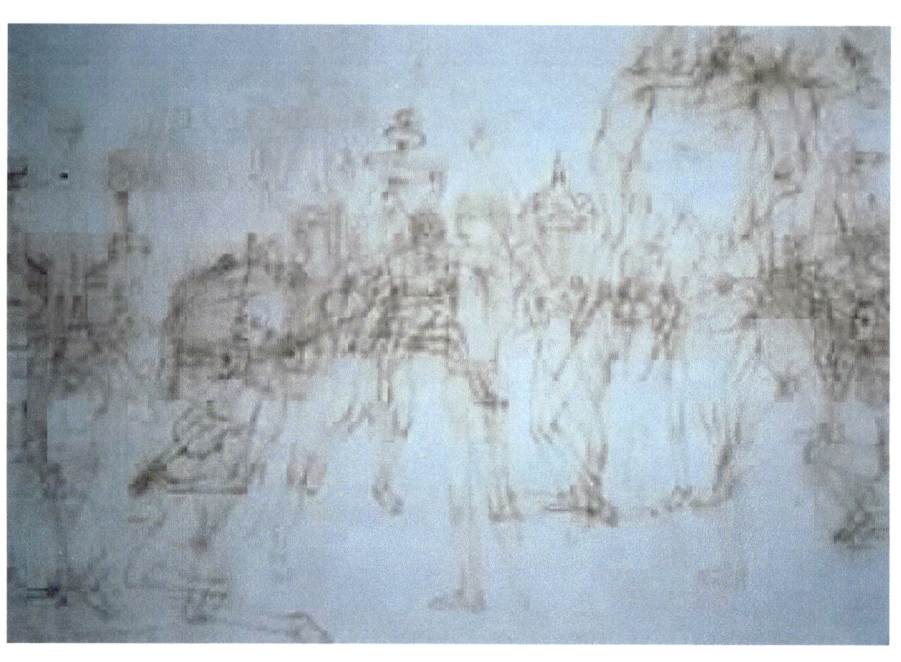

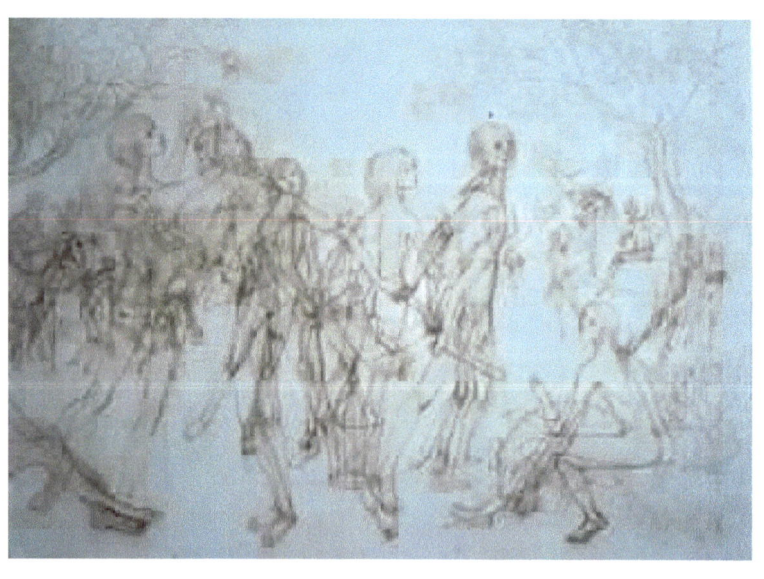

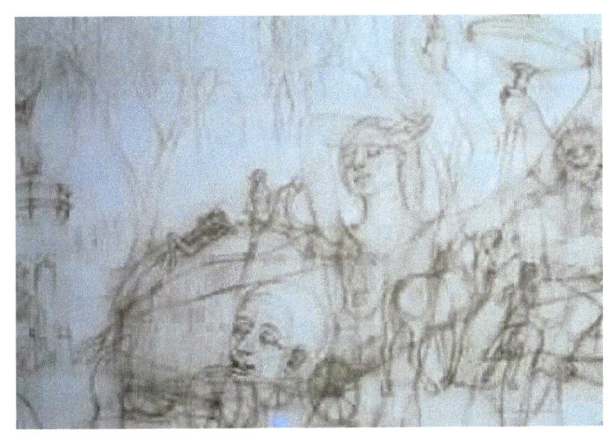
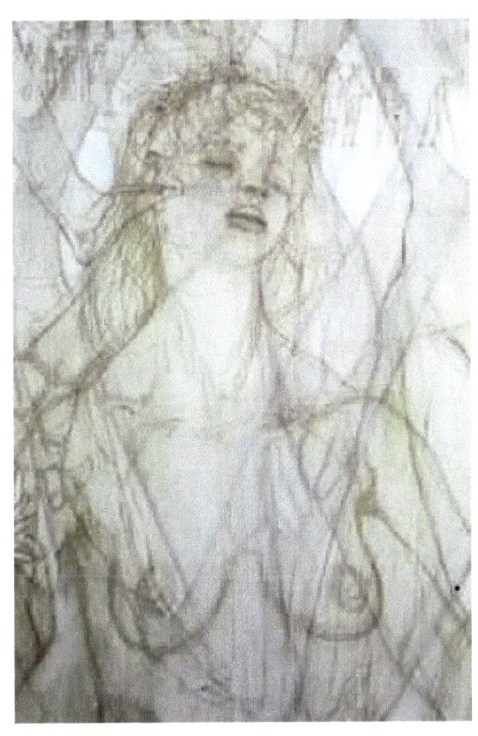

Mural - History of Bridgeport -, Bridgeport Connecticut Library 1984

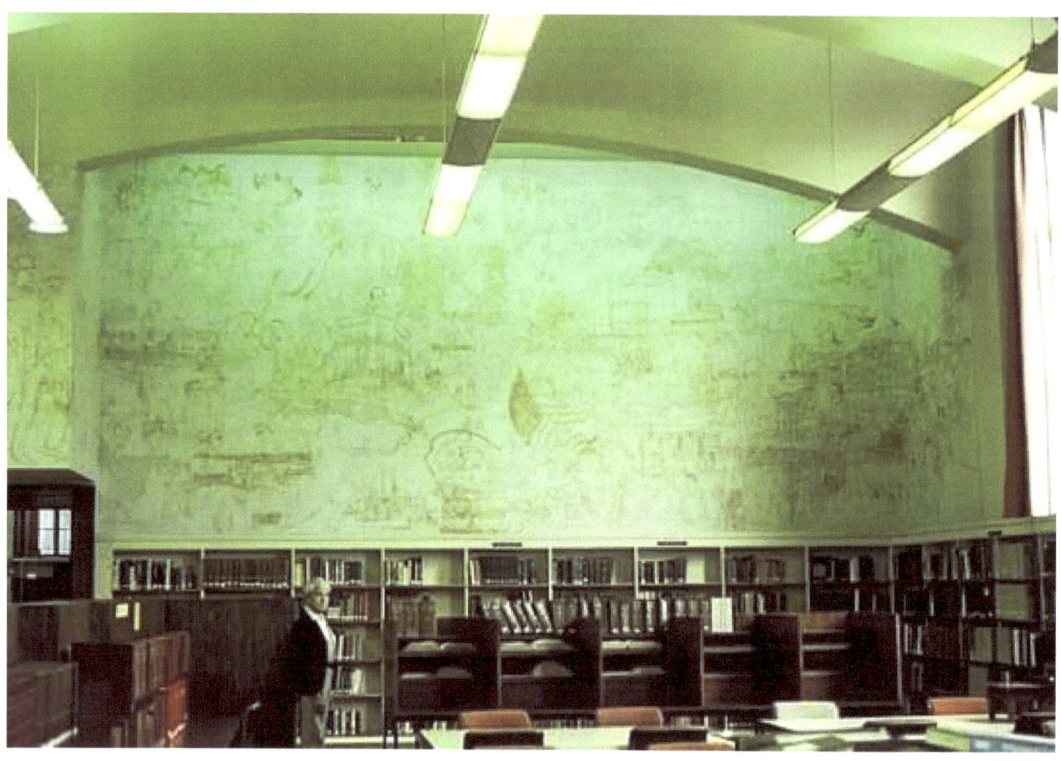

Bernard Riley's final major work, The History of Bridgeport from 1836 to 1936 is in the Bridgeport Public Library, on the wall of the Reference Room. The mural is 40 by 13 feet.

"Well, I was interested more in the character of the city than the people, rather than any heroic kind of mural; one that would show tremendous heavy industry. There was some heavy industry in Bridgeport, but actually the character of the city was more technical. It wasn't Pittsburgh, although there were smelters here and there were iron factories here. The general character of the city was more one of machinists and toolmakers and dye makers and designers. This was the truth, the strength of the city. And I wanted to show the people.

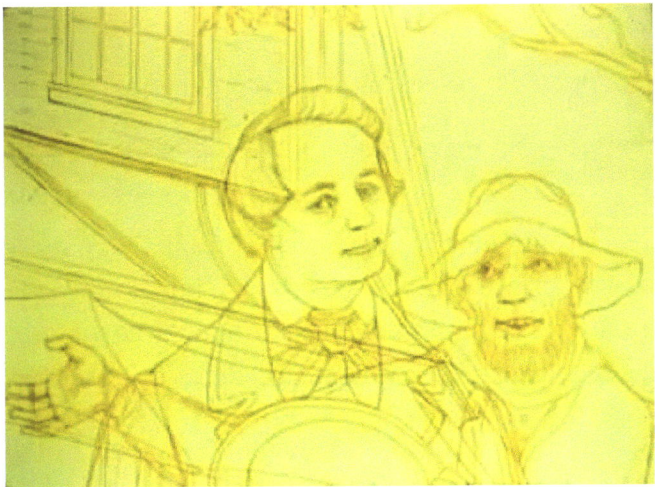
This is Isaac Sherman, the first mayor of Bridgeport talking with a seaman just off a boat in the harbor.

There is Mr. Bullard, who was an important part of the city. And he was in the city of Bridgeport. He started in 1888. And he built a lathe whose design spread all over the world, literally. The computerized lathe that they use today is just basically the same machine.

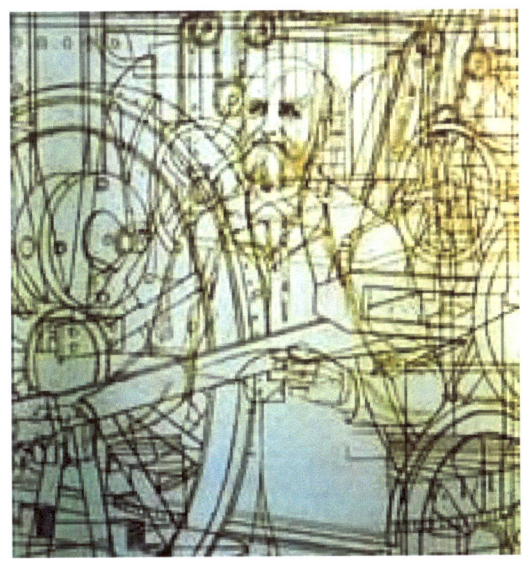

There is a picture of P.T. Barnum and Tom Thumb, on their return from a very successful trip to Europe. Tom Thumb came back to Bridgeport as the "Prince of Bridgeport, which he is known throughout several capitals, where he met Kings and Queens in several countries in Europe. And they came back with a bit of a bundle of money. And they did this special little thing for the Bridgeport Ladies Charitable Society and raised some $300 for their cause.

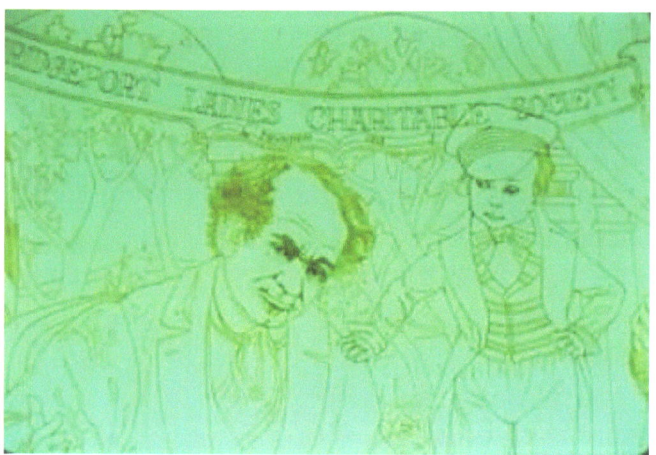

This is a fire that burned out seven big buildings on Water St. To this point, the center of Bridgeport was at Water St. After the fire it moved to Main Street and Fairfield Ave.

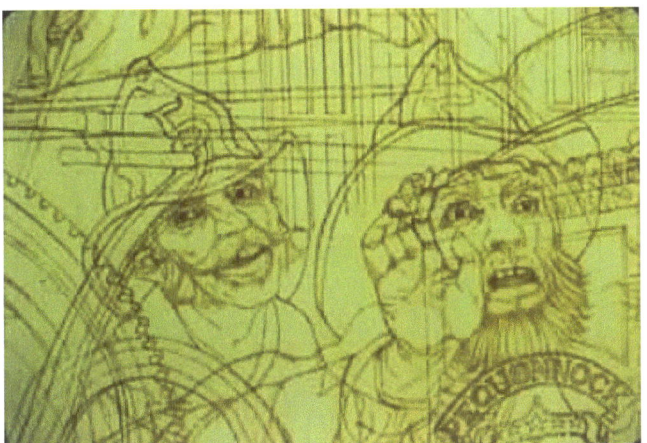

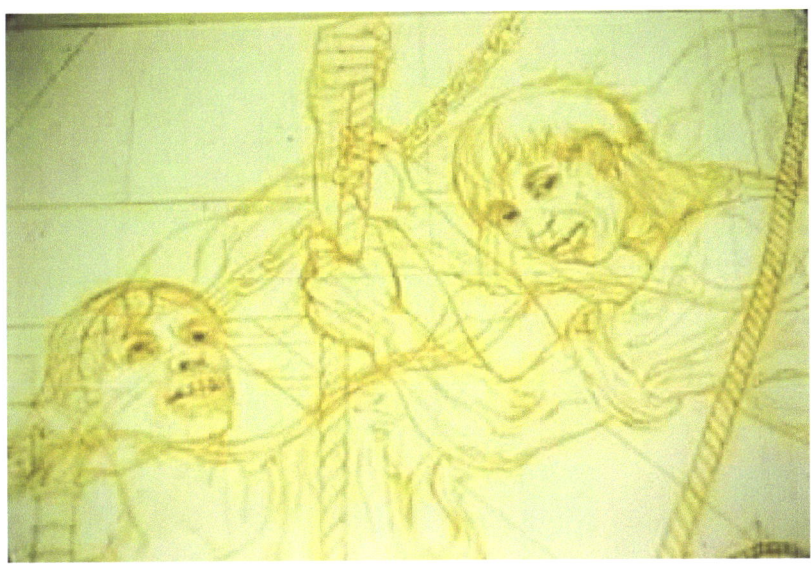

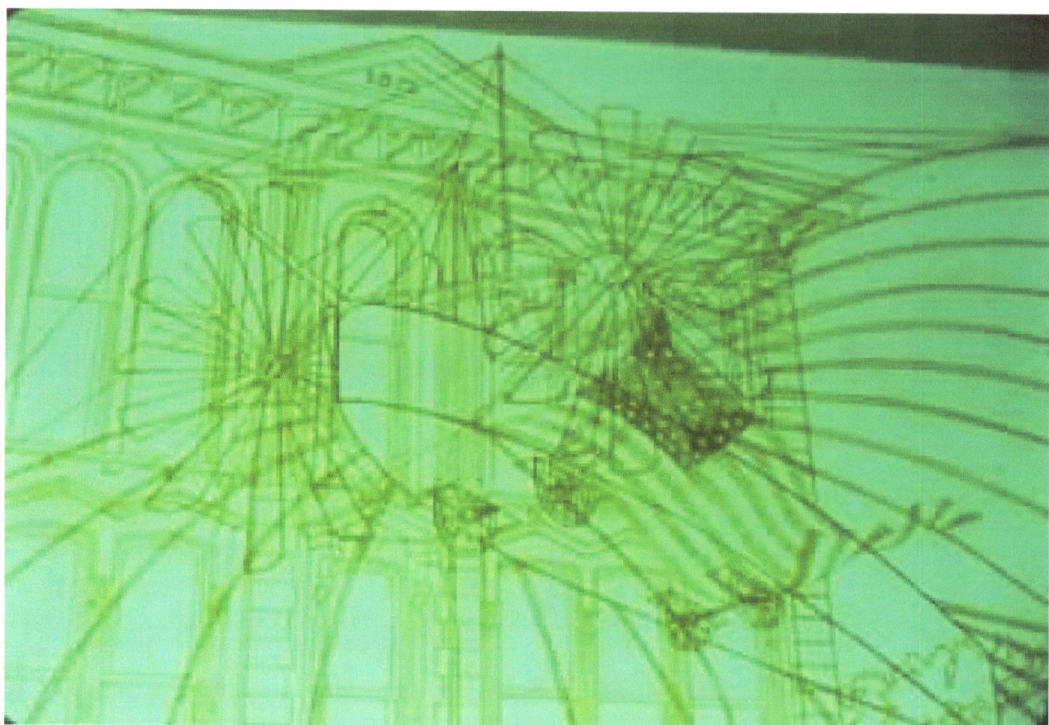

This was this was the earliest of hand powered dirigibles. This was flown in Bridgeport in 1901, which was ahead of the Wright brothers. Gustave Whitehead build a plane that flew in Bridgeport. And there were there's quite a bit of evidence that it did fly

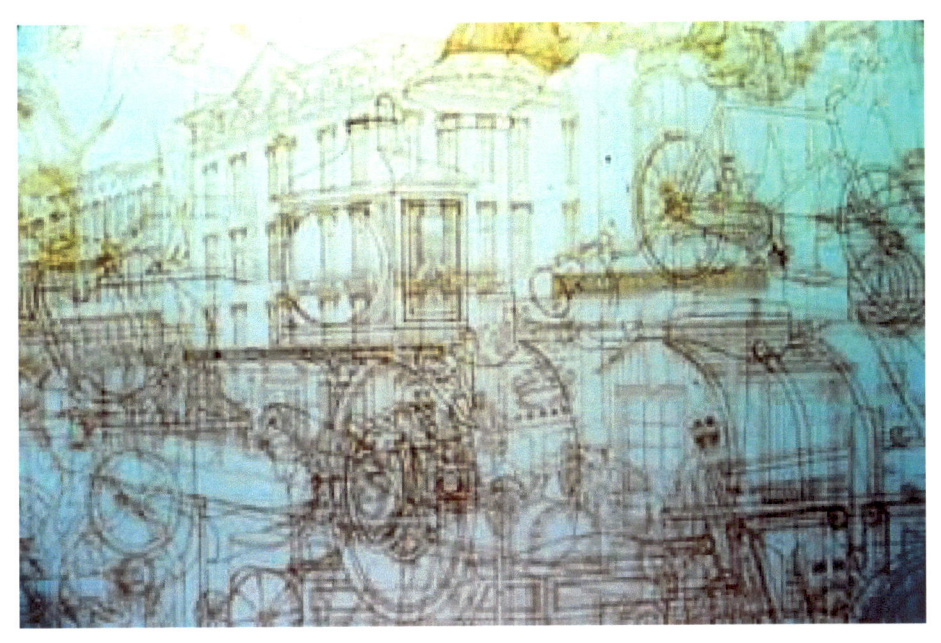

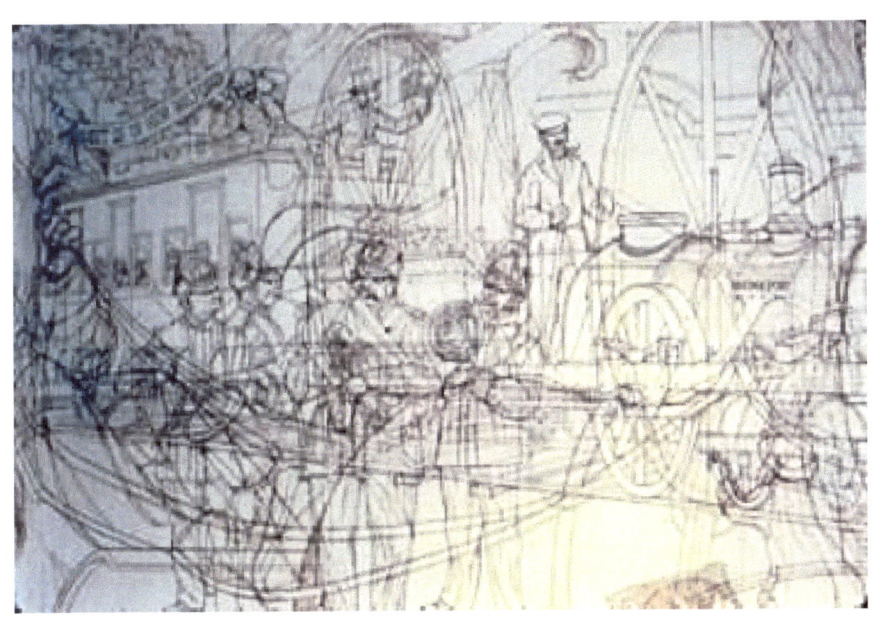

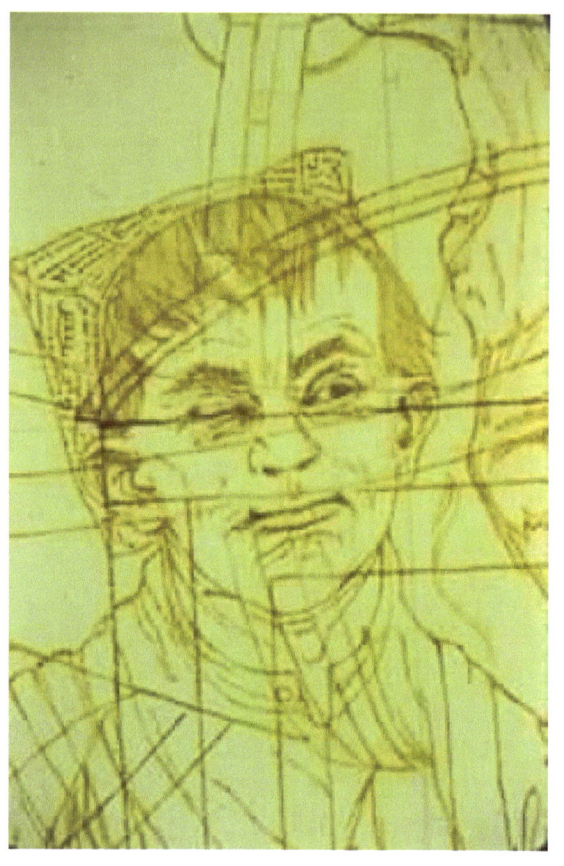

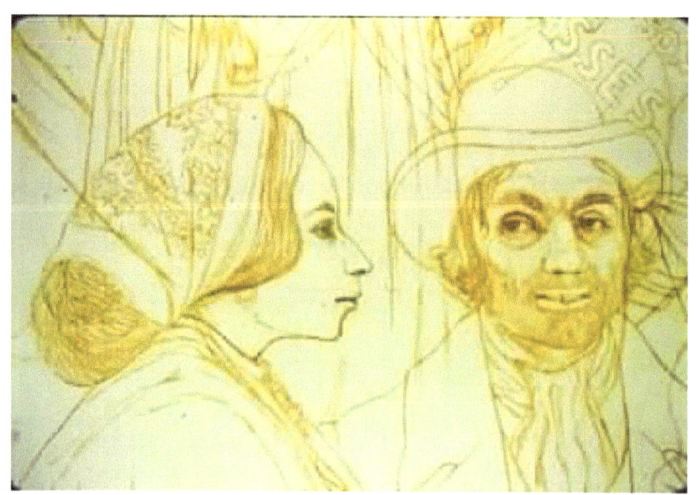

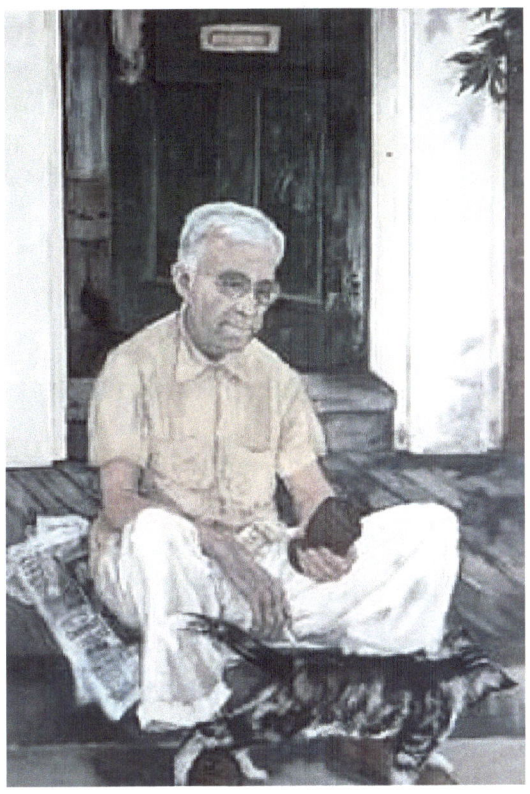

Grandpa - portrait of artist's father John C. Riley holding his woodcarving, His mother Anna Buckley Riley is standing in the doorway 1952

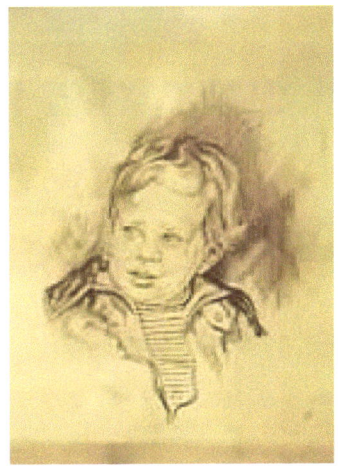

John, the artist's son, age 5

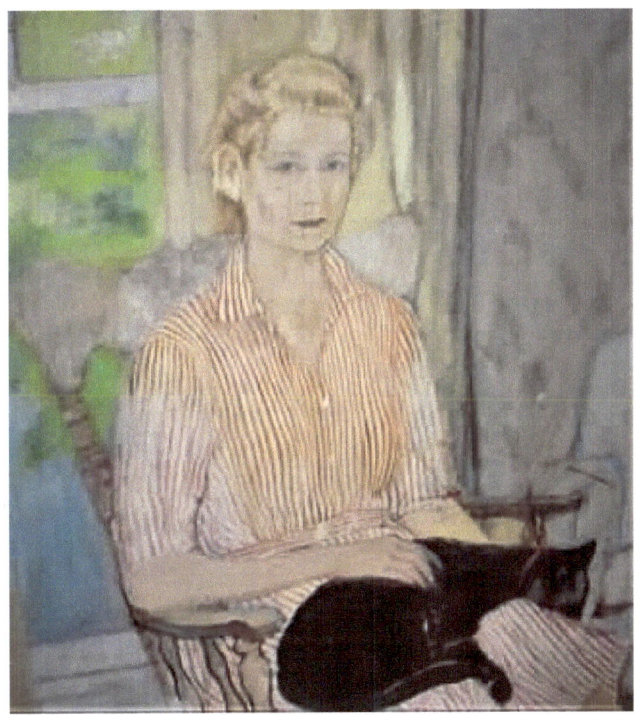

Marie, the Artist's wife

Appendix one – list of major works

Bernard Riley created more than 200 works during his career. This is a list of the major works

Title	Year Painted	Medium	Size
Here's to McGinngan	1942	Oil	18x23
Holiday	1951	Oil	34x28.5
J Street	1952	Oil	29.5x35
The Strikers	1954	Oil	36x48
Grandpa	1954	Oil	32X46
Sleeping Clown	1954	Oil on Presswood	20x30
Not by Bread Alone	1955	Oil on Board	36x48
Man with the Wounded Brid	1958	Oil	47x55
Gonzaga Mural	1958	Oil	84x336
Battle of Anghiari	1960	Oil	40x60
Dancing Mouse	1960	Oil on Masonite	30x40
Seven Men Waiting	1960	Oil	36x48
St. Francis and the Woman Possessed by the Devil	1961	Oil	36x48
Players - The	1962	Oil on Press wood	48x84
Palace of Medici	1965	Oil on Press wood	30x40
Narcissus	1965	Oil on Wood	30x40
Poet with a White Dove	1965	Oil	24x48
Procession	1968	Oil	72x144
Garden of Uffizi	1969	Oil	30x40
Bird Sellers	1974	Acrylic Wall Drawing	82x192
Homage to the Medici	1979	Oil	60x108
Bridgeport Library Mural	1982	Acrylic Mural	480x156

Appendix two - exhibits

Bernard Riley exhibited locally and in many locations around the country starting in Philadelphia when he was stationed there in the Navy

American Academy of Arts and Letters
Bridgeport Jewish Community Center
Bridgeport Public Library
Contempory Arts and Crafts
Detroit Museum of Fine Arts
Eastern States Exposition
Fairfield First Bank and Trust
Fairfield Public Library
Fairfield University
Housatonic Community College
National Academy of Design
New Haven Paint and Clay Club
New York Hilton Hotel
Pennsylvania Academy of Fine Arts
Silvermine Guild of Artists
St. Vincent's Hospital Bridgeport, CT
The Nature Center, Westport, CT
Third Stream Atrists, Bridgeport
University of Bridgport
Wadsworth Atheneum Museum of Art
Wooster School, Danbury CT

www.ingramcontent.com/pod-product-compliance
Lightning Source LLC
Chambersburg PA
CBHW051201220526
45473CB00003B/865